ERIC HOLCOMB

Indiana State Republican
Party Chairman, and
Former Deputy Chief
of Staff and Campaign
Manager for Indiana
Governor Mitch Daniels

LEADING *the* REVOLUTION

LESSONS FROM THE MITCH DANIELS ERA

Published & distributed by:
Traders Point Publishing

in association with:
IBJ Book Publishing
A division of IBJ Media
41 E. Washington St., Suite 200
Indianapolis, IN 46204
www.ibjbp.com

ISBN 978-1-934922-73-6
Library of Congress Control Number: 2012939826
First Edition

Printed in the United States of America

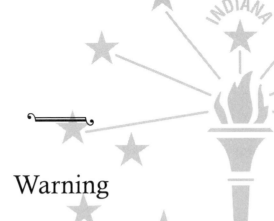

Warning

THIS BOOK IS UNAUTHORIZED. Knowing Mitch would say, "People have better things to do with their time than read about me," I didn't seek his approval. I simply told him I was writing a book and would be talking to his family and friends. I wanted him to hear it from me first. As I expected, he did not encourage my endeavor, considering that we were up to our eyebrows in real work at the time. I did mention, however, that I had been answering the same questions again and again over the last seven years. A modest tome explaining his approach with stories about the process could help others seeking to develop their leadership, regardless of occupation or politics. And besides, I said, midnight to one o'clock in the morning was my personal time to use as I chose.

With a half-smile, he shot back the look we all understood to mean, "I won't stop you. Don't embarrass yourself."

This manual is not just for candidates or elected officials. Many of the examples will also make sense to entrepreneurs and CEOs because the book is about being an agent of change, a leader who gets results. Hard-driving, down-to-earth, intelligent leadership is the difference between success and failure. Mitch proved it. And this is how, in part, he did it.

For Janet

Contents

LEADING *the* REVOLUTION

LESSONS FROM THE MITCH DANIELS ERA

Foreword

No one has had a closer view of Governor Mitch Daniels' remarkable leadership than Eric Holcomb.

Within these pages you'll learn a lot about Mitch and his tenure as Governor of Indiana and why every single elected official – and aspiring elected official – should read this book and highlight its many lessons.

America could – and should – learn a lot from Mitch Daniels.

— Senator Dan Coats

It is somewhat unusual for a lifelong Democrat to have the opportunity and honor to enthusiastically endorse this great brook about Mitch Daniels.

I am so proud of Indiana's Governor Mitch Daniels. He is a brilliant and highly effective leader. A genuinely good guy who is focused on making government work for every citizen, especially those who are vulnerable and need a boost.

Talk is easy. Work is hard. Mitch Daniels is one of the rare leaders who has learned how to master both defining a mission and achieving measurable results in private and public life. His lessons apply not just to those in politics, but leaders of all stripes, in all sectors. He has been successful in both business and politics by following a simple road map — a road map all of us should read, digest and execute. The good news for you, the reader, is that there is no one more qualified to package all these lessons and offer concrete examples of how you can improve your company, government or organization than Eric Holcomb. He learned from Mitch. Now you can learn from them both.

— Mr. Herbert Simon
   Owner and CEO of Pacers Sports & Entertainment
   Chairman Emeritus of Simon Property Group, Inc.

Who is My Man Mitch?

TODAY, CAMPAIGNING AND GOVERNING have become more about settling past scores and less about solving current problems. As the second decade of the twenty-first century unfolds, why are we still talking about past Presidents Clinton and Bush? While George W. Bush campaigned as a uniter, America drifted apart and divided during his eight years in office. We became bipolar, not bipartisan. Vocally extreme characters dominated the political spectrum, tugging and pulling with great effort, but to little avail. The hard left had enough of the far right and vice versa; both sought revenge.

The day after he was elected, fresh-faced junior US Senator-elect from Illinois, Barrack Obama, told reporters "I was elected yesterday, I have never set foot in the US Senate. I've never worked in Washington. And the notion that somehow I'm immediately going to start running for higher office just doesn't make sense. So look, I can unequivocally say I will not be running for national office in four years, and my entire focus is making sure that I'm the best possible senator on behalf of the people of Illinois." Then on *Meet The Press*, January 22, 2006, just one year into Bush's second term, Senator Obama repeated, "I will serve out my full six-year term."

The rest, as they say, is history. Just days later after a verbal about-face, then Senator Obama began crafting a clear message to close Gitmo, bring home the American troops in Iraq, and jump-start a failing economy, hoping to thereby close the Bush chapter once and for all. Obama would lead this hard-charging call for "change" all the way to the White House, racking up the record number of votes ever received by an American president. Within months of taking office and emboldened by sixty Democrat senatorial allies and a massive majority in Congress led by Nancy Pelosi, President Obama doubled down on bailing out banks; fired a private sector auto company executive; hired czars to oversee various private industries; took over General Motors, Chrysler, and the school loan industry; printed and wired money to states to employ local teachers; paid citizens to trade in their old cars; advocated making it easier for workers to unionize; pushed for an energy policy that would have the government cap energy company production; and made his primary legislative goal to expand government subsidized health care, now known as Obamacare.

The excited opposite ends of the political spectrum returned to their deadlocked and shouting ways, and hopeful independent millions caught in the middle became disgusted that the process reverted to form. Today, it is FOX versus MSNBC. Drudge versus the Daily Kos. Rush versus Huffington. Rachel Maddow versus Sean Hannity. A Republican congressman shouted, "Mr. President, you lie," during a joint address to the House and Senate versus a Democrat congressman who stated that Republicans wanted old people to die without insurance. With the two political parties so far apart, the nation ached for reconciliation.

Independents who supported the Obama ticket in droves later wondered if the nation's Capitol could solve any problem, let alone the long list the current Administration targeted. Base Democrats wondered why President Obama had not done more, while Republicans claimed he had done too much too fast. The public at large came to view Washington as a place ruled by a culture of corruption motivated by the same greed and lust for power that brought down Wall Street. The American brand of governance was not only tarnished, it was wounded and on one knee.

In the population epicenter of the country, however, a once reluctant voice continued to be tuned in among all the unproductive noise. How did Mitch Daniels who never wanted the job go on to be that voice? Content with his past public service and his time leading a national think tank, the predictable path would have been for Mitch to return to the private sector where he had most recently helped lead a Fortune 200 company. His keen interest in innovative businesses focused on improving the quality of lives would have been a homecoming difficult to resist. It took a genuine draft movement to convince Daniels and his family to alter their reasoned course. But once convinced, taking the path less traveled, one that guaranteed nothing but hard work and sacrifice, could no longer be refused.

In 2003, Indiana found itself at a crossroads. There were good and well-intentioned people who had been at the helm; however, the state had been floating listlessly on a course to mediocrity during the previous two decades. Indiana was in what Mitch would later call "an all-hands-on-deck situation." In some areas the state had already slid off into unsafe and rocky territory. To expect a different result would require a different type of leader, someone with rigorous ideas and persistent enough to do what it took, damning the torpedoes in order to cure what ailed the state.

A few short years later, America found herself standing at the same crossroads where Indiana once stood. Unrelenting conversation was heard about re-founding and reconstructing the nation. Regenerating America's purpose would require the brightest minds in the country just as it had in the late 1700's, when patriots first established and fought for a united national identity expressed through the genius of men such as Jefferson, Washington, Paine and Franklin. Imagine a present-day Congress filled with inspired American minds, such as: Whitman, Welch, Day O'Connor, Hawking, Gates and Wooden – innovative thinkers, industrial trailblazers, risk takers all loyal to the country that gave their ideas a chance for success.

As a once hyper-partisan operative, willing to tug as hard as the opposition pulled, I must confess that my outlook on what could be achieved through the political process was set on low. Playing defense against one extreme by dialing up the rhetoric of the other, without ever solving any of the nation's systemic problems, was the accepted strategy. Living in a two-year perpetual cycle by definition had a tendency to produce stalemate and at times even a counterproductive Congress. In other words, our Congress had taken on a "Just win today" mentality.

Over the course of nine years working with My Man Mitch, however my belief in our governmental system has been reinforced as I have witnessed proof that it can still work. Mitch eloquently spoke a different political language, one in which ideas, no matter whose they were, remained paramount. One in which right made right. Imagine how refreshing and infectious it would be if others adopted this language.

It is my hope that after reading a few examples of his leadership in action and getting to know his approach to governing better, you might decide not only to be the CEO of your software company, farm five thousand acres, write the next great American novel, discover a cure for cancer, or run your family small business...but that if you want to change the status quo or are reform-minded, you might decide to run for public office or encourage the next leader with character and vision to step forward, just like Mitch did.

Mitchell Elias Daniels, Jr. has often been described as a fearless problem solver, a change maker. His rare blend of intellect, experience, and commitment to public service made him a member of the select group of successful leaders the nation was just getting to know. From an early age, Mitch seemed to be on the fast track to accomplish great things. Born on April 7, 1949, in the steel valley town of Monongahela, Pennsylvania, he was the son of a first generation Syrian American. Mitchell E. Daniels, Sr. Mitch and his only sister Deborah received a clear understanding that hard work and reputation would in large part determine their lot in life, an understanding learned directly from their father, a pharmaceutical company salesman, and their mother Dorothy Wilkes Daniels, of Scottish Irish descent.

Mitch's paternal grandparents emigrated from Syria to Ellis Island in 1905, ending up in Monessen, Pennsylvania. His grandfather, Elias Esau Daniels, known as "Louie" and as Mitch described him, "penniless and illiterate," ran a pool hall and numbers racket, going on one day to "become a benefactor of a hospital in his home village in Syria."

After a year in Pennsylvania, Mitch and his parents moved to Atlanta, Georgia, where his sister was born in 1951. When Mitch was nine, the family put down permanent roots in Indianapolis. He earned his first buck on a neighborhood newspaper route and started to make lifelong friends in the public school system where he would excel. Later, a senior at North Central High School, Mitch was elected president of the student body and, as Indiana's top male graduate in 1967, was named the state's Presidential Scholar and a National Merit Scholar.

Mitch's first exposure to politics was observing his mother, a nurse, volunteer her time to various GOP causes. As a teenager, he volunteered first on an unsuccessful US Senate campaign and then while in college, as an intern in Indianapolis Mayor Richard G. Lugar's office. Working there gave Mitch the opportunity to be mentored by L. Keith Bulen, a man many considered one of the most successful Party operatives in Indiana history. Bulen became almost a second father to Mitch and taught him the value of the kind of organization that separates the great leaders, such as Lugar and Reagan, from all the others. Bulen was known as a Party boss who played hardball and ran his operation like a boot camp.

At Princeton on scholarship in 1970, Mitch had what he called, "an unfortunate confluence of my wild oats period and America's libertine apogee." He was arrested for marijuana possession and spent two nights in the local slammer his junior year, paying a $350 fine for maintaining a common nuisance.

Eighteen years later Mitch told the *Daily Princetonian* that he thought any chances he might have had for competing for public office were shot. To date, he has always disclosed this incident on job applications and even wrote about it in a 1989 column published in *The Indianapolis Star*. He learned early not to hide from a mistake but to take responsibility and learn from it.

The 1960s to the early '70s was a time when college students could defer eligibility for the Vietnam draft until graduating from college, and by the time Mitch graduated, his draft number (147) was not called and the war was winding down. He was awarded a bachelor's degree from Princeton's Woodrow Wilson School of Public and International Affairs in 1971. Right after college, Mitch was appointed vice president of an advertising firm, Campaign Communications, and began working on Mayor Lugar's reelection campaign. Three years after that, he was appointed the mayor's principal assistant.

Mitch then managed Lugar's election to the United States Senate, defeating Senator Vance Hartke by almost twenty points. Mitch joined Senator Lugar as his administrative assistant and attended Indiana University Law School (1975-76). He later transferred and earned a Juris Doctor degree from Georgetown University Law Center in 1979, attending at night while working as the senator's chief of staff from 1977-82.

It was during those early years that one of Mitch's dominant characteristics came under scrutiny. He was unusually frugal. For one thing, his fellow workers noticed him using both sides of his yellow legal pad paper. Another confirmed story while he was working on The Hill was about the time he picked change out of a restroom urinal to buy more beer at the bar. He also drove a beat-up VW Beetle that was not even street worthy.

After Lugar was elected chairman of the Republican Senatorial Committee, Mitch was dispatched to serve as its executive director (1983-84). He restored the financial health of the organization and then joined the Reagan White House as Reagan's chief political advisor and deputy assistant for intergovernmental affairs, serving as a liaison with state and local officials from 1985-87. At that point Mitch left government service to join the think tank world as the chief executive officer of the Hudson Institute in Indianapolis, where once again he restored a multi-million dollar budget to financial health and also worked as a partner in the law firm of Baker & Daniels.

When then sitting Senator Dan Quayle became Vice President in 1988, he turned down a US Senate appointment for family reasons from Indiana Governor Robert D. Orr. Mitch and Senator Quayle became close as he crisscrossed the country, campaigning as George H. W. Bush's running mate. The senate seat would ultimately be filled by then Congressman Dan Coats. In 1990, Mitch bolted for the private sector and signed on as a member of the senior management team at Eli Lilly and Company, headquartered in Indianapolis.

Within three years Mitch was running Eli Lilly's North American operations where he became senior vice president of corporate strategy in 1997. These were the years (1990-2001) of personal and professional development that I heard Mitch most reference and reflect on as the sourse of lessons he learned that best prepared him to govern. He spoke at length about innovation, speed, being part of a competitive team directly involved in improving the life quality of people who suffered, and dealmaking as the exhilarating aspects of his work in the private sector.

In 2000, Mitch agreed to co-chair Congressman David McIntosh's Indiana gubernatorial campaign. Many of the issues raised during that unsuccessful campaign, such as property taxes and spending, went unaddressed and became even more serious problems by 2004, when Mitch would return to state politics.

After more than a decade deeply rooted in the private sector, Mitch's reputation as a fierce fiscal manager had not gone unnoticed at the highest level in the public sector. On a recommendation from a mutual friend, Al Hubbard, President-elect George W. Bush and Vice President-elect Cheney called, asking Mitch to take a leave from Lilly and accept an appointment as the nation's director of the Office of Management and Budget, overseeing the nation's $2 trillion dollar budget. Mitch was nominated by the President on December 22, 2000, and confirmed by the Senate on January 23, 2001. To be confirmed, Mitch, by law, had to liquidate all of his stock holdings, which he did. He then began the regular commute from Indianapolis to Washington, DC.

It was during this second White House tour of duty that he earned the nickname "The Blade" for his dogged determination to cut wasteful spending. His years as the OMB director were eventful and some on The Hill grew to dislike his bluntness. He once said Congress's motto should be: "Don't just stand there; spend something." His office answering machine played, "You Can't Always Get What You Want" by the Rolling Stones. The late, legendary Democrat Senator Robert Byrd of West Virginia called him "Little Caesar" and the late Republican Senator Ted Stevens of Alaska said the only way for Mitch to repair his relationships with Congress was to "Go home" to Indiana.

Mitch's family remained in Indiana while he commuted during the two years that included 9/11 and the ousting of Saddam Hussein in Iraq. On the home front, a Draft Mitch for Governor movement was underway. Running for governor was never an ambition or a foregone conclusion. In fact, Mitch remained a reluctant candidate for all the right reasons, protecting his family from the predictable savagery of the American political campaign process and his commitment to the job he held as the nation's budget director. People in Indiana had different ideas.

Through the Draft Mitch for Governor movement, folks in every county logged on a Draft Mitch website and encouraged him to run and business and community leaders FedExed hundreds of letters of support to Mitch's Washington office. After the familial concerns had been addressed and his job in the Bush Administration reached a point at which he could honorably depart, Mitch announced in early May that he was stepping down. He then returned to Indiana to answer another call to launch another campaign, this time and for the first time, his own for governor in 2004. On June 9, he formally tossed his hat in the ring by filing with the State Election Division.

The primary field was crowded when Mitch made the decision to run, but a few bowed out and quickly endorsed him. State Senator Murray Clark became Mitch's campaign chairman. Another endorsement came from State Senator Luke Kenley, a veteran fiscal policy advocate.

Of the two primary opponents who remained, one failed to get the number of signatures required to run and the other was unable to raise money outside one wealthy supporter. All the while Mitch continued to raise backing from the party faithful as well as from many first-time contributors to the cause, another important indicator of growing support.

His Democrat opponent went after him from his marijuana use in college to his personal finances. One of the funnier incidents during the 2004 campaign occurred when Democrat legislative leaders stood on the State House steps, holding a press conference on Mitch's "drug use." When a reporter asked if any of them had ever smoked marijuana, one by one they admitted they had. That day marked the last day they tried to hunt with that dog.

Even vicious commercials about Mitch's stock holdings rang hollow when the facts were laid out for public consideration. Through it all, Mitch remained disciplined and never ran a negative ad against his opponent. So, in stark contrast, all the mud flew in one direction. Without realizing it, the opposition helped define Mitch as the candidate who always took the high road.

While honing his Spanish speaking skills, Mitch crisscrossed the state nonstop in a green and white decaled RV covered with thousands of supporters' signatures. During the journey he regularly penned little ditties about the people he met, places he visited, and lessons learned. He emailed them to his My Man Mitch volunteer base as the campaign unfolded, pre-the age of Twitter. Later he compiled and published them in a book form titled *Notes from the Road* to offset part of his transition expenses to governor.

On November 2, 2004, Mitch Daniels became the first gubernatorial candidate to defeat an incumbent in Indiana (by fifty-three percent), the first Republican governor in sixteen years, and the first governor from Indianapolis. Bringing with him a majority in both chambers of the State House. When he took the oath of office on January 10, 2005, and became the forty-ninth governor of Indiana, he was handed a dysfunctional state government, including a $700 million deficit, and $760 million in back payments owed to schools, universities and local governments.

Not one to rest on his laurels, Mitch was reelected on November 4, 2008, to a second term. He won by eighteen points (fifty-eight percent) and received more votes than anyone who had ever run for office in Indiana, capturing a total of 1,563,873 votes. He won throughout the entire state, not just in Republican leaning areas, taking 79 of 92 counties in 2008, as opposed to 2004, when he won 73 and tied two against his incumbent opponent. Despite the anti-GOP hurricane force headwinds in the 2008 election cycle, Mitch not only won, he won big: fifty-eight to forty percent.

The race was called two minutes after the polls closed. Mitch had even won his opponent's home rural county and the county where she grew up. Hoosier voters sent the clear message that they viewed Mitch as a change agent and reformer who gets results. The next day's *Indianapolis Star* headline read "Not Even Close."

After his first term, many initially believed his reelection race would be close because the bold way Mitch governed led some voters to feel he was doing too much, too fast. His 2008 opponent was a former congresswoman supported by experienced, left-leaning organizations, such as the Indiana State Teachers Association, the Service Employees International Union, EMILY's List, the National Education Association and the impressive investment President-elect Obama had made in Indiana. Obama spent millions of dollars on continuous television ads, starting in the primary, employed hundreds of field staff and visited Indiana over forty times. His effort paid off, as he won the state, the first time a Democrat nominee for President had done so since LBJ in 1964.

Keep in mind: more people voted than ever before in Indiana state history. Voter turnout exploded on college campuses and urban areas where many were first-time voters. Like Obama, Mitch was supported on these campuses, where vote centers increased even more county turnout. Mitch won every age demographic, including the eighteen to twenty-nine-year-olds, by nine points (fifty-one to forty-two percent). Those young adults were nineteen percent of the Indiana electorate in 2008.

Seniors sixty-five and older were his strongest demographic, supporting him by thirty-six points (sixty-seven to thirty-one percent). This was a nineteen-point improvement over 2004, when Daniels lost voters sixty and over by two points (forty-eight percent to fifty percent). Mitch got twenty-four percent of Democrats, enjoyed a thirty-eight-point swing with independents from 2004, capturing fifty-seven to thirty-nine percent of independents. He received twenty percent of the African American vote, won fifty-eight percent of men voters and fifty-six percent of women, effectively showing he had no gender gap in support.

The Mitch coattails and resources carried the two other statewide candidates on the ticket by running television commercials with both candidates, conducting get-out-the-vote phone calls to "support the Daniels team" and utilizing his campaign organization to turn out votes specifically for the other candidates. While Mitch won by nearly 500,000 votes, Greg Zoeller was narrowly elected attorney general by just 38,865 votes and Tony Bennett was elected superintendent of public instruction by 50,944 votes.

People asked, "How did you do it"? In short, Daniels won big in such a tough environment because of his leadership. Hoosiers connected with his steadfast vision and work ethic. Voters recognized his expertise in diverse areas, such as attracting a record number of new and diversified jobs to the state, dramatically reducing homeowner property taxes, and organizing an effective response to the severe weather and record floods in the summer of 2008. What made My Man Mitch unique, however, was neither his extraordinary professional achievement nor the opportunities life had presented him. His commitment to public service balanced by his insistence on leading a grounded private life made Mitch a rare human being who was able to connect with folks from all walks of life.

He served as an elder at Tabernacle Presbyterian Church in Indianapolis, where he had attended since he was ten, and co-founded The Oaks Academy, an inner-city Christian school that promoted academic excellence and racial reconciliation based on religious principles.

In 2008 Mitch described the school as, "It is the living witness of what can happen when people of God search for the right way to let God act through them…and unite as believers, who believe in children and who believe in the One who made those children." He went on to say that, "Of all the things life has brought, this project is the most important human endeavor I've been privileged to be a part of."

He had been a trustee, director, and supporter of the Goodwill Industries of Central Indiana, the Freedom House, the Fund for American Studies, the Lynde and Harry Bradley Foundation, and a founding member of the Friedman Foundation. At the time of this writing, he is serving on the Board of Trustees at Western Governor's University and on the Board of Trustees of The Hunt Institute for Educational Leadership and Policy.

Throughout both his campaigns and as governor, Mitch continued to stay in homes, not hotels. His overnight hosts achieved the highest status in the organization and were affectionately referred to as his "roadies." He was a motorcycle fanatic, owning two Harleys, one black hog and one detailed with an Indiana flag theme. He rode with friends on sunny days and sometimes in the rain. He could quote you any line from *Animal House* or *The Godfather*, answer any question about the Dodgers (Brooklyn or LA), and quiz you on the most obscure facts about seventies rock and country bands. Asked for his favorite top ten list by WKLU, he submitted:

1. "Brown Sugar," Rolling Stones
2. "The Breeze," Lynyrd Skynyrd
3. "Subterranean Homesick Blues," Bob Dylan
4. "The House Is Rockin'," Stevie Ray Vaughn
5. "20th Century Fox," The Doors
6. "Strange Brew," Cream
7. "Jemima Surrender," The Band
8. "Katmandu," Bob Seger
9. "Born on the Bayou," Creedence Clearwater Revival
10. "Connection," Rolling Stones

*Cheri loved the annual State Fair and was competitive in axe
throwing, cow milking and watermelon seed spitting.*

He walked his bearded collie named Nigel around the neighborhood, preferred what he called "real" not "light" beer, and is one of the most quick-witted guys you would ever meet. Through the power of technology, he remained in constant contact with lifelong friends from grade school to college to his buddies scattered throughout the evolution of his various careers. Annual golfing trips and getaways to places such as the Dodgers camp, kept Mitch in touch with those who knew him best. In fact, Mitch even stayed in contact with his inspirational ninth grade English teacher, Mr. Watson.

In 1978, he married his lifetime sweetheart Cheri Lynn Herman Daniels and they have four daughters, Meagan, Melissa, Meredith and Maggie. He always remained humbled by the long list of accomplishments by those who were closest to him, his family. Their sense of humor proved the apple did not fall far from the tree. I'll never forget the first time I heard one of his daughters say, "Dad, you just crossed the dork line."

His wife, Cheri, was the granddaughter of the legendary baseball hall of famer Billy Herman, who played with the Chicago Cubs and Brooklyn Dodgers before serving in WWII, and then went on to play with and manage other teams. The Dodgers just happened to be Mitch's favorite team. Cheri, along with their girls, always have maintained their private lives. They have largely stayed away from prop politics that all too often goes with campaigning for high office. As First Lady of Indiana, Cheri eased into her self-defined role and protected her privacy. She chose her causes carefully and was passionate about each one. Hoosiers respected that.

To say she was not the typical political wife would have been an understatement. As witty as Mitch, Cheri was his equal. Her smile and comebacks were as memorable as her grace. One of

Cheri's favorite things to do was spend time being a ham on local radio shows.

Turning 63 did not slow Mitch one step (except for the rotator cuff and knee surgeries) and he was in better shape than most who might read this book, certainly than the one who wrote it.

He practiced the healthy living he preached. A typical ten-day workout schedule included: Day 1 – mile swim, Day 2 – 5¼ mile run and weight training, Day 3 – mile swim, Day 4 – 40 minutes elliptical trainer, light weights, Day 5 – day off, Day 6 – mile swim, walking (code for golf), Day 7 – mile swim, walking, Day 8 – day off, Day 9 – mile swim, Day 10 – 5¼ mile run, weight training.

Before Mitch, if you had asked anyone what Indiana was known for, you would have most likely received the answer home of Larry Bird or the Indy 500. After Mitch was first sworn into office on January 10, 2005, Indiana became a national leader known for efficient state government, solving problems without raising taxes, and creating good paying jobs even during the toughest economic times. Indiana became known as a place that was different, an outstanding place to live, work, and play.

From New York to California, Mitch's passion for necessary reform and results was infectious and the single reason those around him were inspired to remain loyal to his efforts. The following chapters describe how Mitch took Indiana from failing to first and document some of the steps he, his team, and the people of Indiana took together.

Before you take off or touch down, know your plan.

ONE

Plan Your Path to Victory

THE MOST IMPORTANT TASK that a business, organization or campaign can undertake to be successful over time is to articulate a clear mission that is understood by everyone. To weather the challenges ahead, a solid foundation of values and goals needs to be established early. Both Mitch For Governor campaigns printed the mission, passed it out to every staffer, and posted it in every office.

Campaign battlefields are littered with wealthy losers and the best-looking or smartest candidates who fell short against political neophytes because they simply did not communicate a clear mission. Beyond the campaign itself, economies fluctuate, the electorate is moody, global issues shift the public's focus, and the competition always has something to say about you. But do not expect to be flattered. Everyone had better be prepared to give persuadable answers to the following key questions.

- Why are you running for this specific office?
- What do you want to accomplish?
- And, why should we join and follow you?

It has been said, "We become what we think about, who we associate with, and accomplish what we plan." If you see yourself as the leader, ask yourself, "Who is following me, where am I leading them and why?" If you cannot answer these three basic questions and share your passionate vision, do not expect others to devote their time, treasure and talent to helping you. And, if you have not personally reviewed and endorsed your campaign or business plan, do not expect your employees to.

From the first day on the trail, Mitch Daniels said his number one priority would be job creation and increasing the net disposable income of Hoosiers – in other words, increasing upward mobility for everyone. At his announcement for candidacy on July 7, 2003, outside Hinkle Field House at Butler University, Mitch plainly articulated the mission:

> *"We aim for growth in jobs and incomes, for a transformed Indiana economy featuring more high-growth, homegrown businesses, a richer mix of enterprises, and a reinvigorated, higher-margin agricultural sector."*

To be sure, you must always have supporting priorities that strengthen your mission's message. Mitch went on to add the specific goals necessary to fulfill the mission:

> *"We will aim for constant improvement from our public schools, never resting until other states routinely compare their results to ours. We will improve access, affordability and quality*

of health care in Indiana, while encouraging and helping Hoosiers to take greater charge of protecting and promoting their own health. We will establish higher requirements of openness and ethical behavior throughout state government, and put in place new systems to uphold and enforce them…"

After his 2008 landslide reelection victory, he again laid out his vision in his second inaugural address. Mitch also described the new Hoosier spirit that had been evolving as a result of efforts during his first term to address and realize needed improvements on all fronts: fiscal, jobs, education, healthcare, and ethics.

"Best of all, a new mentality has taken root, a new boldness born of risks successfully run and change successfully delivered. In overwhelming numbers, Hoosiers have declared that we are unafraid to lead, to try the new before others do, and that we like the results of doing so.

"No more will historians write that we are backward and out of step. That we are, at best, "gradualists" who prefer to keep to 'the more secure edge of the river.' The Indiana they depicted would never have led the nation in capturing international investment, cutting and reforming property taxes, or bringing peace of mind to those without health insurance. That Indiana would never have devised a way to build public infrastructure in record amounts without a penny of taxes or borrowing, or to liberate the new infrastructure of fiber and frequency in a nationally innovative way.

"In dramatic contradiction of old stereotypes, Hoosiers have announced emphatically to a world that belongs to the creative and nimble, where fortune truly favors the bold, that we not only accept change but are prepared to lead it, and invite the rest of America to follow us."

The key to burning your mission message is to have it always ready for consumption by the supporters you are asking to help you realize it. Think of your core mission message as the hub of a wheel with other priorities serving as spokes that support and strengthen it.

- Solid infrastructure attracts businesses to locate and grow.
- Attracting better paying jobs leads to an average statewide increase in income.
- Healthier, better-educated citizens will make Indiana a more attractive place for businesses to locate.

Associates, staffers, and volunteers should not only promote your campaign or company line, they must know it. To know it, they must own it. Again, for them to own it means you have to publish and repeat it often. In Mitch's case, we published a *Road Map for Indiana's Comeback* in both the 2004 and 2008 campaigns. The *Road Maps* were the same size and printed just like standard folding state road maps, front and back. A great deal of strategic thought went into these folksy maps.

Initially Mitch wanted to keep the plan simple, a sound approach when you are playing it safe in order to win; when you are thinking: do not make a mistake and do not lose the lead.

But as his travels increased, so did his awareness of new problems. Issues specific to local communities, unknown to outsiders of one community or another but ultimately important to the whole state, were added to his to-do list. Those travels showed that many problems had been swept under the carpet for years, which caused folks to become fed up or worse, cynical. To keep his plan simple would have meant to further ignore these newly exposed agenda items, leaving them for someone else's watch. To include them added breadth and depth to his agenda. So, the popular "Keep It Simple Stupid" (KISS) approach was replaced with a more comprehensive one that basically said, "If you elect me, I will go to work on these seventy-four specific ideas; now hold me accountable."

With his campaign 2004 *Road Map* in hand, Mitch's first-term record and Indiana's story started to get noticed around the country. One, the transformation of a status quo state government to a "leaner, cleaner taxpayer friendly government," as Mitch put it, started paying dividends. After the 2005 Legislative session, session, of the seventy-four legislative and executive branch initiatives on the 2004 *Road Map*, fifty-nine passed, five partially passed and nine were enacted through executive action.

In Mitch's case, having the *Road Map for Indiana's Comeback* meant he earned a reputation as an idea generator. Holding this position created its own defense. When the opposition's negative attack machine geared up, we stayed positive. Multiple headlines told the story of opponents who ran negative ads against Mitch's agenda even though they did not offer an agenda themselves. Voters appreciate a clear agenda, even if they do not agree with all of it. Ideas are paramount and many times make the winning difference.

Because we had been a heavy policy staff during the first campaign, we researched every state agency and identified both shortcomings and strengths. During the research phase, policy teams worked with private sector experts so when it came time to fill key leadership positions, we had a long list of atypical talent to contact that would be better equipped to endure the "we've always done it this way" entrenched government pushback that lay in waiting. Because of Mitch's different approach that included nongovernmental input, the transition was swift and smooth.

Every coach has the plays called before his team steps onto the field. You, too, should have your playbook ready on day one.

Immediately, from the day Mitch took the oath of office, he began dismantling broken pieces of state government and rebuilding them with a contemporary structure. He first improved the state's business environment by reorganizing an antiquated Department of Commerce into a vibrant public-private partnership now known as the Indiana Economic Development Corporation (IEDC), in which the governor would serve as chairman of the board. This new entity began to capitalize on the state's market position at the crossroads of America by updating concrete, fiber, and wireless infrastructure networks that had become uncompetitive.

Mitch insisted on key changes so Indiana could, as he said, *"act at the speed of business, not the speed of government,"* in attracting new jobs.

Faster than anyone imagined, Indiana became one of *"the best sandboxes in America,"* as Mitch would always say, in which entrepreneurs could create jobs. But it took many steps to attract the world's attention to this new jobs magnet in the midwest.

One of the steps was passing the Indiana Telecommunications Deregulation Act, which became another national model. Indiana's telecom reform provided high speed internet service to the most rural parts of the state, increased competition among carriers, which resulted in lower prices, and created thousands of new jobs.

Already a longtime player, Indiana became a national leader in agricultural production, for which Mitch received the Excellence in American Agriculture Award. The state also grew as a leader in alternative energy. In a few short years, Indiana became the number three leading state to install E85 gasoline pumps, a leader in the production of green energy, home to the largest wind farm in the eastern United States, one of the fastest growing wind farm states in the country, and home to one of the largest soybean-based biodiesel production facilities in the world. Construction of the world's first commercial scale, integrated gasification combined-cycle clean coal plant was also begun.

Indiana initiated a Shovel Ready Program, allowing local governments to pre-permit properties, including many brownfield sites in inner cities, to ensure less red tape and streamline marketing efforts to speed up development. Working with the Department of Defense while other states continued shedding jobs due to the Base Realignment and Closure (BRAC) process, Indiana not only saved thousands of jobs at Crane Naval Warfare Center but also added a thousand new jobs in Lawrence where the US Finance Center, Department of Accounting and Financial Services and Department of Defense were located. On top of this, the state secured Army funding for Muscatatuck, a massive urban training center to better prepare soldiers for combat.

With zero inventory taxes already on the books in Indiana, Mitch's first term resulted in capped business property taxes, lowered workers' compensation costs, tax credits for research and development, patent income exemption, and incentives for venture capital and headquarter relocation prospects to invite companies to consolidate their multi-state operations and investments to Indiana. Now, state government agencies all work together to create jobs, not slow them down.

For example, when Medco Health Solutions, a Fortune 500 pharmaceutical company by-mail distributor, was looking to expand operations, a neighboring state told the company time would be necessary to accommodate its specific requests.

In Indiana, however, the nimble Indiana Pharmacy Board called an emergency meeting and quickly adapted its permitting and licensing requirements for Medco. When Honda looked to build a new factory, bringing 2,000 jobs to the state, getting the state's Department of Transportation to add a new exit ramp off a major interstate was as affordable as it was feasible.

For the record, during its first year, the IEDC closed more deals than the previous two years combined, and in tough economic times more than fifty companies with business in both Indiana and other states decided to consolidate their operations to Indiana.

During his governorship, Mitch regularly traveled to Japan, Korea, China, Germany, and England to thank job investors in Indiana and recruit new ones, as all governors must. It paid off: in 2006, Indiana was the only state to attract three new auto manufacturing facilities, including Honda, Toyota and Cummins.

At the same time Mitch also created the Office of Management and Budget (OMB) to grade agencies and root out lingering inefficiencies. To be sure, there remained a constant healthy tension between the OMB and all other state agencies that prevented silos from sprouting again. Government programs that did not work were exposed and corrective action assigned. Agency budgets that were completely spent did not automatically get resubmitted plus three percent every year. Wasteful spending stopped. Creating the OMB in 2005, however, was not enough. Eventually, software was created to build a checking system that balanced all accounts on a daily basis. Updating antiquanted software will eventually expose past and current problems. Do not avoid change out of fear it may embarrass you; embrace the potential improvements and always audit your systems.

In addition to these safeguards, long overdue ethics reforms were passed, and an inspector general post was created to actively root out fraud and waste of tax dollars. Mitch immediately targeted all the low-hanging fruit and eliminated expenditures on items, ranging from $170,000 spent on two cookbooks produced at taxpayer expense to the $8.2 million paid annually to Kentucky to guard Indiana prisoners. Eight mail rooms, seven print shops and nine sign shops, some right next to each other in the state government building, were consolidated. Mitch trimmed over $250 million in unnecessary spending and saved a total of $190 million by just renegotiating over thirty of the previous administration's contracts.

The state employee rolls were reduced by more than twenty percent through attrition, reorganizing, and outsourcing government functions to the more efficient private sector. These changes contributed to the lowest number of state employees since 1975, and the lowest number of government workers per capita in the nation.

Mitch also sold off two-thirds of the state's aircraft fleet and more than 2,000 surplus state cars and brought in hundreds of millions through a one-time tax amnesty program, more than four times the predicted amount. After two years, the governor authorized a modest pay raise for state employees (although not for himself) and instituted a pay-for- performance program. With the government fat cut away, the core mission could be better supported.

Have a timeline for every initiative.

Because the first road map was so popular, we decided to print them regularly even during legislative sessions. Road maps were mailed to supporters and always available on the website for easy review and transparency.

Road maps will help you with your annual planning. It is good to be anxious but keep in mind that you have more than one year to accomplish goals and that your customers will respond to your maturation. So, first things first. For instance, pay off debt, build a healthy reserve for tough times, attract jobs, and then you might be able to lower taxes. Many candidates claim they want to cut taxes right out of the gate, with no mention of services that will have to be eliminated because of the lost revenue.

For example, Mitch strengthened Indiana's state fiscal health by paying off the state debt owed to local governments, schools and universities. Having erased the state deficit and having cut spending, he announced over a billion dollars in reserves.

For the first time since 1996, Indiana passed four consecutive balanced budgets. During his first session, he slowed state spending growth from six percent to less than two percent per year, passed the tightest two-year budget in fifty-five years, all with no new taxes, building a foundation that maintained Indiana's excellent fiscal standing.

Results get noticed.

Mitch had already gone in swinging hard at overspending during his earlier stints in Washington, DC, as White House Budget Director and Director of the Office of Budget and Management. In 2002, Americans for Tax Reform presented him a Hero of the Taxpayer award "for his relentless efforts to control the federal budget."

The Citizens Against Government Waste also applauded Mitch for bringing "a fresh new approach to the position of OMB Director." They went on to say, "Mitch Daniels worked tirelessly, often facing an uphill battle, to break Washington of its pork barrel spending habits....Taxpayers should truly be grateful for the service that Mitch Daniels provided this country."

After Mitch took the Indiana governor's oath of office in 2005, the Tax Foundation's *Business Tax Climate Index* ranked Indiana number one in the Midwest; the Milken Institute ranked Indiana number one in the *Cost of Doing Business Index*, and the *Forbes Report* said Indiana had the sixth lowest cost index in the country. Both CNBC, July 2008, and *Site Selection* magazine named Indiana as the most improved state for business in the nation. *The CEO Magazine* rated Indiana number one in the Midwest and now number five in the nation as a top location for doing business.

Michael Hicks, Ph.D., director of business research at Ball State University said, "Indiana sits as a small island of growth in the Midwest...." (*Indianapolis Business Journal*, Dec. 24-30, 2007)

Since 2005, international companies have committed more than $5.7 billion to their Indiana operations and more than 13,000 new jobs. Indiana ranked number one in North America in the creation of production jobs through foreign investment in 2006 (*IBM 2007 Study*). *The Wall Street Journal* pointed out that Indiana led the nation in 2010, with nine percent of all new private sector jobs; quite an accomplishment, considering the state represented only two percent of the nation's population.

In October 2008, Governor Daniels was recognized by The Manhattan Institute's Center for Civic Innovation for his innovative policy initiatives and one month later was named Public Official of the Year for achievement in government service by *Governing* magazine. Later he received the inaugural Excellence in Innovation Award presented by Rose-Hulman Institute of Technology.

Rose-Hulman President Matt Branam said, "Using his business experience and creative approach to government, Governor Daniels has implemented a number of programs that have resulted in financial stability for Indiana. At a time when states across the country are struggling, Indiana is now one of the top states in the country in terms of business attractiveness."

In late 2010, The Hudson Institute honored Mitch with its Herman Kahn Award for his creativity and visionary leadership and in January, 2011, he received the first FISCY Award, a nonpartisan award for fiscal discipline and leadership, along with Senator Kent Conrad (D-ND) and Congressman Paul Ryan (R-WI).

"The people of Indiana must realize that what our state has in Governor Daniels is something that we haven't had in decades – a reformist working in the capital who has created a balanced budget, a stable, fruitful economy and reduced state spending in the process...." (*Ball State Daily News*, August 22, 2006)

"Daniels has been extraordinarily successful at implementing innovative and effective public policy. His inventive, results-driven approach has been complemented by genuine fiscal discipline...." (Mark Hemingway, *National Review*)

"(He) is driven by the very Republican notion that a more efficient government can save taxpayers money." (Lou Zickar, Politico.com)

After balancing the books, create the environment that is competitive and offers certainty to stakeholders, then work every day to improve the service of the operation you were charged to oversee. Mitch proved government can work better with less and should be flexible enough to spend more when an important need is identified.

Mitch next turned his eye to retooling government to enable it to better serve the taxpayers who fund it and to attract new businesses seeking to operate in a predictable government environment. In 2008, Indiana achieved a AAA credit rating by Standard & Poor's for the first time in state history.

Keep your message easy to understand.

During Mitch's first term, the former governor, Joe Kernan, and then Indiana Supreme Court Chief Justice Randall Shepard, led a commission to review the way local government operated and then submitted ways to reform or modernize.

The commission took roughly a year to travel around the state, and held town hall-like forums with stakeholders to discuss potential changes. Commission members ultimately presented Mitch with twenty-seven ideas for making Indiana's governing bodies more efficient. Only one problem. Because the commission had so many recommendations, the public and legislators had difficulty comprehending and prioritizing the *Kernan-Shepard Report* list. Four years into promoting local government modernization, only a third had been accomplished to date but advocates continued to keep beating the drums of reform.

Years three and four in Mitch's first term brought the commission's recommendations which contained more local government reform ideas than ever in modern history, into the conversation. These initiatives reached into all ninety-two Indiana counties and challenged the way local government had operated since before the Civil War.

"When it comes to the structure of local government, Indiana skipped the twentieth century. A time traveler from Civil War days would be dumbstruck by an iPod or I-70 or eye surgery, but he would have no trouble recognizing our system of local government.

"We have too many offices, too many taxing units, too many politicians, too many of everything, and they all cost money." (Governor Mitch Daniels, *2008 State of the State Address*)

And so, in 2008, Mitch pushed many of the twenty-seven ideas recommended by the bipartisan commission.

Mitch did not just focus on spending tax dollars better, he set out to allow taxpayers to keep more of their income in the first place. For instance, in 2007, the Tea Party movement had already been expressing itself in Indiana. Citizens garbed in eighteenth century colonial costumes threw tea in a city canal, protesting unfair property taxes and marched on the Capitol.

While previous state and local leaders had kicked this can down the street for years, Mitch led an effort to constitutionally cut and forever cap all Hoosier homeowners' property taxes at one percent of a home's assessed value, leading the fight to pass fair, far-reaching and final property tax relief. Average homeowners, seniors and young families alike, saw a thirty percent cut in their property taxes, the biggest overall tax cut in state history. Indiana now has one of the lowest property taxes in America, a reduction in the corporate tax rate from 8.5% to now 6.5%, and an automatic tax refund when the state surplus grows too high.

Mitch said: "Not only are we entering a new era of taxpayer protection, but this ushers in a new era of reform in Indiana and makes our state the nation's leader in defending and promoting the American dream of home ownership."

Any dynamic leader must be able to articulate why changes will make life better. Mitch explained in detail how a leaner, cleaner government better serves its customers, and in this case, taxpayers. He always asked, "If the private sector is providing a service and the competition can be found in your local yellow pages, why should government try to take a piece of the market share?"

Paying off debts and having a savings account improves your credit rating, making your state or company more attractive for future job investment, which in turn leads to higher employment.

Understanding the layers of entrenched bureaucracy of any centuries-old organization is paramount. Do not expect good ideas to convert from dream to reality just because it makes sense to you; neither should you believe that stakeholders can reform from within if incentivized appropriately. Making it attractive to change, meaning this properly functioning department or that level of government will receive more funding, often goes further than simply starving the beast.

And lastly, be prepared to agree to disagree. Rarely will everyone agree one hundred percent to a list of proposals. Such was the case with Indiana's original twenty-seven recommended local government reforms, which included abolishing the local sheriff's office in all ninety-two Indiana counties. The sheriff is often the most revered and trusted local elected official. Reassigning his responsibilities to another office might have made dollars and cents sense, but this idea never earned any traction because it was not one of the reforms the governor and others were passionate about.

Play through your team's strengths and weaknesses; your opponent will.

You must know what your competition knows. Mentally play your plan through, like a game of chess, before you step into the public arena. Think two or three moves ahead and know what lurks around the debate corner. Getting advance feedback on your strategy will prepare you to meet the public that is going to devour and react to every detail. You do not want to learn how your plan could fail at a press conference as you are unveiling what you considered your next brilliant idea. Welcome constructive criticism because if you do not, you will pay the price of operating in a vacuum.

In fact, it is wise to keep a threat chart and update it accordingly. Someone should be tracking all the soft spots in the organization, where improvement needs to occur, what problems continue not to be solved. What is the media and/or your opponent focusing on? If you do not think you have any vulnerability, you are not paying attention to the competition, you have become complacent because of past victories, or you have just simply lost your objectivity. All three can be deadly to future productivity.

Star athletes always believe a younger guy is out there, working harder than they are to be the best. The hunter is always the hunted in business, sports and politics! Keeping a simple, constantly updated pie chart on how the press, public and your competition are criticizing you is an honest way to track the major issues requiring your attention outside of running the organization.

Lastly, envision and be able to articulate what your state's or company's destiny is.

Your plan lays out the path to achieving your goals. The size of the problems you face must equate to the boldness of your action. If your state is floundering near the bottom of the national list of high school graduation rates, figure out how many more students you want to see graduate the next year, then in four and eight years. Figure out how to measure the rate of annual improvement so you can plan for change and make the tools for improvement available to students and teachers. Mitch described it as follows:

> "We offered ourselves as people of change. We urged our fellow citizens to aim higher, to expect more from our state government, but also from our schools, our businesses and, ultimately, from ourselves. We tried to hold up the prospect of an era in which we would leave behind old arguments for new solutions, provincialism for unified purpose, timidity and caution for boldness and even risk-taking, all with the goal of restoring our state as a place of prosperity and promise.
>
> "We said plainly what kind of change we would bring. The policies we will pursue have been in full view for months. When I leave here today I will sign executive orders making the first of those changes, effective immediately. On arrival at the people's house, I will personally deliver those of our proposals that require legislative approval to our new partners in the Indiana General Assembly.
>
> "And, eight days from tonight, I will propose, as a part of my State of the State presentation, approaches to the fiscal emergency in which we enter Chapter 49. We will waste no energy assigning blame for this crisis, and we must waste no time in addressing it. Our actions must be bold, because the problem is huge. They must touch every individual and interest, because they must be fair, and adequate to the challenge at hand." (*2005 Inaugural Address*)

The international language for "Good morning" is "Can I warm you up?" You think this guy told a few friends who poured his coffee that morning at the local diner? Small gestures mean big things in communities, no matter where you are in the world.

TWO

Always Be People Purposed

THE SYMBOLIC BACKDROP WHERE Mitch first announced he was running for governor in 2003, was not lost on anyone paying attention. Butler University's Hinkle Field House was home to one of the most famous high school boys' basketball state championship games ever played. Millions have seen the movie *Hoosiers* in which a small rural high school underdog not only challenged but prevailed against incredible odds in 1954.

After his long awaited kickoff announcement, Mitch boarded the Indiana-built RV, known as RV1, where he would spend the next sixteen months on the road, going places no gubernatorial candidate had visited in years, if ever. His first stop would be Scottsburg, a small bucolic county seat in southeastern Indiana, where he connected with voters and ended the day at a brats and burgers cookout in Milan. If there was one secret to Mitch's success, it was that he kept it real ever since that first stop at the Scott County Courthouse. He was the most accessible governor

Indiana had ever seen, having visited all ninety-two counties at least three times by the end of the first campaign.

His point of view always oriented itself from a taxpayer's perspective and that was validated on election night, 2004. Voters appreciated his preference to travel the state in an RV or on his Harley Davidson motorcycle and his insistence on staying overnight in Hoosier homes, not in hotels. There is no substitute for old-fashioned road time and training, where Mitch said he got "his instructions."

Any leader will tell you there is no shortcut to success, and building relationship loyalty is no different. Mitch continued his travel practice even after being reelected, always appreciating that last hour before lights out, talking to his overnight family hosts about issues on their minds.

Mitch's commitment to learning made him the best at one-on-one retailing, not just in campaigning, but more importantly, in governing. Mitch told the story about talking to former Tennessee Governor, and now US Senator Lamar Alexander, about his mode of travel to which Lamar replied, "It will probably make you a better candidate, but it will certainly make you a better governor."

This travel also provided invaluable on-the-ground intelligence so there was no use for an entourage or Washington, DC, veteran consultants. There was never a need to translate the conversations that took place in the feed mills or board rooms because Mitch himself spoke the language and was personally connected to the topics discussed.

Truly connecting with the people and issues of the state enabled him to personally write the scripts for all campaign commercials and delivered speeches. His overnight and travel investments allowed his words to resonate. As with the speeches and writings of great past and present leaders, such as Abraham Lincoln, Winston

Churchill, and Nelson Mandela, Mitch's words are powerful in part because they are born out of genuine experience. On a Mitch campaign, there was no posing in front of an American or Indiana flag, no studio shots with cute kids or with models in hardhats. The only traveling staff, two recent college graduate "roadies," armed with a camera and note pads guaranteed that every photo of faces and places was authentic, real time, and archived.

And lastly, the travel regime gave the campaign time to evolve naturally as people became aware of the man, trusted the candidate, and got enthusiastic about helping Mitch turn around the state.

Becoming known as a man of the people cannot be bought or contrived. People have to be able to relate from their gut and those authentic encounters, photos, and video interviews communicated realness that no sound bite or talking point could ever convey. The travel personalizes your end goal no matter how big the city or small the town, and your experiences become your natural narrative.

One day Mitch shot me a brief Blackberry email from the road in Verne, Indiana. He wrote, "Verne has been captured without a shot being fired. I have decided that Blue Jeans Bill Williams may have come back as me. What's next?"

"Blue Jeans Bill" Williams was rumored to have been the last governor to visit Verne, Indiana, back in the late 1800s, before Mitch rode into town in March of 2008.

There is no substitute for road time (scheduled visits and impromptu stops).

Going where you are not expected is not only disarming to folks, more importantly it is illuminating to the candidate. Mitch learned countless lessons on the road, such as visiting

Harps on Main in Rising Sun in southeastern Indiana. The owner, William Rees, hand makes world famous harps, a small business he started in his garage. As it turns out, the lady in the store told Mitch, harp music is played in hospital neonatal units because live harp music, in particular, can sooth a premature infant's breathing. Call it musical medicine one string at a time. Road travel is where the reasons for running become real and relatable, where the story is written.

The opposite of being people purposed is flying into city airports to hold press conferences, asking supporters to turn out to watch you regurgitate talking points to reporters. It is pre-packaged and often stale, something you expect from a fast food joint, not from someone you want to trust to guide the future of your state or company.

I heard folks say a thousand times, "He's one of us." In conversation, Mitch was always intently focused on the person and the subject. No looking over your shoulder, scouting for the next vote. Not only did he listen, he was processing the conversation, bouncing it off past encounters. It was not unusual for him to ask multiple questions several layers deep. Then, out came his paper and pen. He personally wrote down contact information and the subject and afterward, there was follow-up from him directly or his staff, many times both. He insisted on one hundred percent follow-up, even if it was to respectfully disagree. Equipped with the facts, he set out only to solve the problem, not blame it away, no matter how simple or complex.

Life on the road put Mitch in more hazardously humorous situations than most governors or multinational corporate executives face in a lifetime – such as being gummed by a hog or bitten by a family's dog startled by the Harley. After one such dog bite, Mitch got a tetanus shot and shrugged it off, saying, "It bled for awhile and took a little medical attention." Bit by a dog on the campaign trail, no big deal. This candidate connection was picked up by the press and public alike.

"Instead of giving a speech in a suit and tie, he met supporters in a button-down shirt and slacks and listened to what Jasper County residents had to say." (*Remington Press*, Rensselaer, 8/6/03)

"Daniels ran a superb campaign, spending almost 18 months on the road in RV One, getting to every part of the state at least twice. He connected easily with Hoosiers and it's obvious by the vote totals that his message of change resonated well with the average voter. The direct, personal contact had to be the most significant factor in his victory." (*The Truth*, Editorial, Elkhart, 11-4-04)

"The image of RV One rolling down Main Street will join the Hoosier political lexicon. The always above-board message that imprinted a favorable Daniels image on voters should be the modus operandi for future campaigns." (*Indianapolis Business Journal*, Editorial, 11/8-14/04)

"It was clear at the onset that Mitch Daniels was prepared for the job of Indiana governor. Gracious and intelligent, Daniels set out 18 months ago to make himself known in each of Indiana's 92 counties." (*South Bend Tribune*, Editorial, 11-4-04)

"Traveling all over the state in an RV was a brilliant political tactic, helping him overcome the traditional bias against Indianapolis. The travels also have given Daniels a depth of knowledge of each corner of the state." (*The Indianapolis Star*, 11-7-04)

"Daniels owes much of his gubernatorial victory to the people he met and listened to during his 56,000-mile odyssey throughout the state." (*Lafayette Journal and Courier*, Editorial, 11-10-04)

"In the end, we've witnessed the first modern incumbent governor to go down in defeat and the first new governor from Indianapolis...ever, and he did it by forging a bond with the folks in the small towns. It came after much toil, sweat, and tears. It has become an epic chapter in our history." (Brian Howey, *The Howey Report*, 11-19-04)

Build roads once only dreamed of and know the power of road recon.

I'll never forget the time early in the 2004 campaign at an event in the northwest quadrant of Indiana when a gentleman informed Mitch that Indiana's past transportation plan was a sham. He said the Department of Transportation (DOT) had no way to pay for all the projects promised to local communities even though they remained on the books. Sure, promises were made to appease locals, but when it came time to start work on new roads, the project was always delayed for some reason, usually lack of funding.

So there was the problem: new roads and bridges were urgently needed with no money to pay for them. After researching the question of how to honestly build (not promise to build) new major infrastructure projects, the answer turned out to be multiple choice:

A. Increase the gas tax
B. Bond or borrow more money and pay for it later
C. Think of something new

Although A and B were not Mitch's approach, option C, leasing a failed government-run state asset to an experienced private sector operator became an attractive option. Although leasing such assets is a common practice in many places around the world, the idea was viewed as foreign-thinking by predecessors. Specifically, the northern Indiana Toll Road built fifty years earlier had not been paid off and was losing money.

By leasing its operation to a private entity through the Major Moves infrastructure building program, Indiana became the only state in the nation to have a fully funded ten-year transportation plan. Mitch negotiated the seventy-five-year lease of the state's only toll road to a Spanish-Australian consortium for $3.85 billion up front. This was the same 157-mile toll road that had been losing money for years under the old state-run patronage management model.

It was estimated that the lease payment brought in two to three times its value. In addition to the negotiated payment, the consortium agreed to invest billions in the toll road operated by them but still owned by the state and to include building a new state police post along the road. Indiana earned more in interest on the unspent funds than the toll road generated in the previous fifty years.

The Major Moves program not only created new jobs and fueled economic growth, it eliminated the inherited $2.8 billion transportation deficit. The deal paid for 104 new roadways by 2015, with 1,600 lane miles. By 2012, the plan had completed two hundred new vital state road and bridge projects and two hundred preservation projects, sent tens of millions of dollars to each county the toll road ran through, distributed just under $200 million to all other counties for their local projects, and created a future transportation project fund, all without raising taxes or borrowing.

While other states were faced with the choices of not building roads, raising taxes or bonding to build, Indiana had the money in the bank, earning interest and ready to move forward on a decade of infrastructure priorities.

Imagine your state building a public toll road in 2010 and still owing on it in the year 2060. Try selling that up front. In contrast, in just 117 days, Indiana negotiated, signed the deal, paid off its debt and became the only state in the nation with such a long-term infrastructure road plan, all with the deposited $3.85 billion balance earning interest for the state.

Some projects, such as I-69 linking southwest Indiana to Indianapolis and beyond, had been studied and talked about since the Korean War. Finally, promises were replaced with ground-breakings and completed under budget.

While on the road, Mitch bumped into folks who could not believe Indiana got such a good deal and solved such an exasperating problem. Sometimes just asking people what they thought was enough to calm their anxieties. In this case though, Mitch solved the problem.

Every state grapples with the cost of the uninsured as well as the cost of insuring state employees. One approach is to grow government and pay for more coverage. Mitch took a free market approach and offered Health Savings Accounts for Hoosiers who previously did not have coverage. These accounts would be managed by the consumer, not the government. In addition to addressing the uninsured, Mitch went after the cost of insuring the state's workforce.

In 2007, Mitch signed market- and patient-centered landmark health care legislation called the Healthy Indiana Plan (HIP) that provided over 130,000 low-income, uninsured Hoosiers with coverage. The plan promoted health screenings, early prevention services, smoking cessation treatment, and entrusted Hoosiers to become value-conscious consumers of health care. It also provided tax credits for small businesses that created qualified wellness and Section 125 plans. The plan was paid for by increasing the state's tax on cigarettes.

In a September 15, 2007, *The Wall Street Journal* columnist, Fred Barnes quoted Daniels and commented, "A consumption tax on a product you'd just as soon have less of doesn't violate the rules I learned under Ronald Reagan."

HIP helps those who cannot qualify for Medicaid to enroll in a plan to which the state contributes up to $1,100 per person (sliding scale) to a Health Savings Account (HSA). Eventually ninety percent of the state government workforce was also enrolled in a high deductible plan with an HSA.

"When I was elected governor of Indiana five years ago, I asked that a consumer-directed health insurance option, or Health Savings Account (HSA), be added to the conventional plans then available to state employees. I thought this additional choice might work well for at least a few of my co-workers, and in the first year some 4% of us signed up for it.

"In Indiana's HSA, the state deposits $2,750 per year into an account controlled by the employee, out of which he pays all his health bills. Indiana covers the premium for the plan. The intent is that participants will become more cost-conscious and careful about overpayment or over-utilization.

"Unused funds in the account—to date some $30 million or about $2,000 per employee and growing fast—are the worker's permanent property. For the very small number of employees (about 6% last year) who use their entire account balance, the state shares further health costs up to an out-of-pocket maximum of $8,000, after which the employee is completely protected.

"The HSA option has proven highly popular. This year, over 70% of our 30,000 Indiana state workers chose it, by far the highest in public-sector America. Due to the rejection of these plans by government unions, the average use of HSAs in the public sector across the country is just 2%.

"What we, and independent health-care experts at Mercer Consulting, have found is that individually owned and directed health-care coverage has a startlingly positive effect on costs for both employees and the state." (*The Wall Street Journal, Op Ed,* Governor Mitch Daniels, March 1, 2010)

"What he did in Indiana, state employees now have health savings accounts and that saved both the state and employees on their health care costs." (Iowa Governor Terry Branstad)

In addition to those covered, over 270,000 Hoosiers qualified for free or discounted prescription medicines through Mitch's Rx for Indiana program. Indiana became a national leader in providing health insurance coverage.

And, Indiana also got healthier by improving its childhood immunization ranking, moving from forty-first to fifteenth in the country. Its obesity ranking improved from first in the nation in 2003, to twenty-eighth six years later. *Forbes* had placed Indiana seventh in the top ten states to improve their obesity ranking in the past twenty years.

As a public safety measure, Mitch has promoted a state-funded regional firefighter training program. Local courses enabled volunteer and full-time firefighters from across the state to learn, practice, and become proficient in the latest procedures for fire control and rescue.

Mitch said, "These devoted men and women have incredibly dangerous jobs and we are thankful they are always ready to respond in our time of need. These lessons provide the best training available at locations that are close to home."

Not only did Mitch solicit ideas from the road, he asked his state agency heads and policy advisors to do the same.

Indiana's statewide fabric is a typical midwestern population sampler with lots of diversity. Spend day one in a steel mill in Gary just outside Chicago; day two in the melon capital of the world in Oaktown, population under 1,000; day three in Madison along the Ohio River; day four in the capital city of Indianapolis, a national convention destination; and day five in Lawrenceburg outside Cincinnati. You will have met native Hoosiers, Russian immigrants, Muslims, physicians, Vietnamese American citizens, teachers, Amish people, Jews, farmers, artists,

Bosnian political refugees, African American students, computer programmers, cooks and caterers, Irish Americans, mechanics, Catholics, Mexicans, roofers and bricklayers, Protestants, foster parents, cat lovers, and on and on.

The breadth of the contrasts in these diverse groups brings a fascinating mix of intelligence, experience, and common sense that requires treating every constructive idea as a strength born out of that different perspective. Mitch taught his lieutenants to value different and competing input, to get out of the limestone building offices, to encourage spot bonuses for good work, and foster a work environment in which everyone recognized that there were just so many days to address the long list of priorities and may the best idea win, wherever it came from.

Be genuine no matter where you are.

Every region of the state heard a consistent message. Mitch told audiences in northern Indiana that they had to be an engine in Indiana's comeback for northern Indiana to succeed; southern Indiana needed to do the same and so on. Indiana was not unique in having to cater to multiple out-of-state media markets (Chicago, Cincinnati, Louisville and some of Michigan); however, when Mitch spoke about economic development, he talked about how we were one team, all in it together, each bringing diverse assets to the table. The only return he promised a financial contributor was hard work and the certainty of good government.

Because of his constant travel during both campaigns, Mitch agreed to let two people follow him around and film his interactions. Both as candidate and later as the governor, Mitch was never allowed to edit or even preview any of the twenty-four episodes of Mitch TV. This reality show aired on cable stations, attracting a cult-like following and disproving any attack that he was out of touch with everyday Hoosiers.

People got to know him as My Man Mitch, which branded the campaign. I have always called this move "checkmate." Mitch TV was one of the campaign innovations that helped achieve its recognition as the best-run 2008 gubernatorial campaign in the country, and as Mitch said … it was not even his idea.

We knew voters would see through a candidate who appeared too rehearsed and always on stage, and Mitch TV proved that he wandered Indiana unscripted. In fact, it might have even exposed a few rough edges, and even that trumped being too polished.

People want to know that you can relate to them, not them to you. They want to know you serve on jury duty when called, you get your flu shots, you buy fresh produce from a roadside farmer, and that it comes naturally to pour another man's coffee, not always have your cup filled.

They want to know you are not above them and can connect to their lives. During the first campaign, I recall the day Mitch yelled for us to stop and pull over as we were passing a house with a permanent flea market in the front yard and on the porch. Walking up to shake the owner's hand, we could not help but notice the grease board on which was written: "Bush lied, troops died, and the rich got richer." The man in front of us, Democrat Precinct Committeeman David Chandler, had written those words. Most Republican candidates would have just driven on by, which was duly noted when Mr. Chandler said, "Mitch, I'm glad you stopped by. If you hadn't, I'd have talked about you."

Share the credit for the good ideas you have learned from others.

Mitch insisted his campaign commercials share the "slices of reality" he picked up along his travels. By committing to this habit, the benefits were twofold. One, people became active participants in the conversation to make Indiana a better place to live, work and raise a family. And two, every idea could be improved upon. This is what you want, citizen input and ownership. It is why every company wants feedback on its product so it can make improvements. It is why Steve Jobs and Apple were so successful. Consumers became the innovators of the ever-improving product. After each idea was presented for public consumption on Mitch's watch, suggestions would pour in from even the most unlikely places. Have the system and staff in place to receive all the constructive criticism that flows in, and welcome it.

Mitch always talked about rebuilding Indiana, many times from the steps of his Indiana built mobile office, RV1.

Meeting people, like buying produce, is a job best done by yourself.

Tarmac press conferences would have never allowed
Mitch to overnight in hundreds of homes across Indiana,
state park inns and even in an old fire station.

THREE

Create Your Own
Conventional Wisdom

CREATE YOUR OWN CONVENTIONAL wisdom; do not let it define you. Too often candidates seeking office rely on outdated institutional knowledge and are unwilling to take the less traveled path.

Conventional wisdom tells you to (1) make a list of your friends and foes, (2) assemble the "usual suspects" as they are known in the business, or veteran campaigners, and (3) conduct a poll to find out what is on the minds of voters.

While experience and corporate knowledge are helpful, they should not dictate how you reach out and develop your team. Determine what you want to accomplish and accept that sometimes you must turn conventional wisdom on its head.

- Conventional wisdom tells you business supports Republicans and union labor supports Democrats.

- Conventional wisdom tells you to campaign and message where your supporters are and focus on turning out only your traditional voters.
- Conventional wisdom tells you to talk about one, two, or maybe three poll tested issues; otherwise voters will drown in the multiple waves of messages.
- Conventional wisdom tells you to first run for local office, then state office, then national office, thereby building your name identification and recording your leadership. In short, there is a grooming process; follow it.

While all that may have been true during the height of party power and lack of instant information-sharing, conventional wisdom is no longer the rule. So, throw those old rules out the window. They should not direct your approach when it comes to seeking support. In fact, turning conventional wisdom on its head can be a liberating and responsible way to replace outdated, even antiquated, ways.

You might be surprised how fruitful it is to trust your judgment based on your instincts as opposed to how others have worked on the same problems for years, locked into the same old ways of thinking.

So, build your own compass and remain true to the trail you seek to blaze. Chances are you will be hitting on the key themes anyway, such as jobs, the economy, and taxes. And if you travel perpetually, you'll run into problems that never appear on polls, such as meth addiction, childcare reform, and the need to clamp down on deadbeat dads. Your experiences will develop your course.

Ideas, facts and substance matter. Do not be afraid to communicate them creatively.

Most reelection campaigns show the candidate in motion, suitably attired in a plaid shirt or coat and tie, cutting ribbons and holding babies. Follow that spot by sprinkling in a few key newspaper headlines and employing a voice talent that doesn't come cheap, emphasizing improvements made on your watch.

In 2008, Mitch decided to take a different route and instead aired a commercial with no voice over, no announcer, no candidate, and no precedent to imitate. The result was sixty seconds of accomplishments, flying at you reminiscent of the beginning of *Star Wars* when the text scrolls up in the opening scene.

It all started when Mitch said, "I want to drown them in facts in sixty seconds." We internally called this spot KICK ASS I, and, because sixty seconds was not enough, we created KICK ASS II. Kick Ass went on to win a national award and was imitated outside Indiana. It was still being requested by candidates at the time of this writing.

The commercial appeared to be on fast forward with unforgettable music; once heard you it, you could not get it out of your mind the rest of the day. Imagine a soundtrack similar to *Pirates of the Caribbean* on steroids. There were those, including me, who thought that if a strong bass voice did not announce the list of accomplishments, the message would never be communicated, certainly not delivered.

I am the first to admit the opposite proved true. We received more email feedback from that commercial than at any other time during both the 2004 and 2008 campaigns. People wrote in saying they loved the music and appreciated the fact that the commercial was factual and positive. High school band teachers wrote us, asking what the music was so their kids could learn to play it during half time at football games. We heard from voters in Kentucky, Ohio, Illinois, and Michigan, saying they wished their candidates would be as positive.

Do not rely on polling to dictate your direction. It is good to learn from it, but build your own compass.

Had Mitch Daniels stuck to a poll-driven script, there was no way he would have learned firsthand about Indiana's struggle with the multiple adverse ramifications of methamphetamine addiction or about the desperate need for hundreds of additional state child protection advocates.

Regarding the former, almost every state in the nation was grappling with all the crime and safety issues surrounding meth production. On visit after visit, frustrated Republicans and Democrats, horrified parents, spouses, county jail personnel, and elected officials at every level of government sought to do something about the effect meth was having on both Indiana's rural and urban communities. A lot of good ideas were proposed, but a master plan and the synergy needed to hit this abuse fast and hard were lacking.

By taking copious notes on the subject and organizing a collaborative effort, Mitch got Indiana to adopt practices focused on eradicating meth production, such as requiring drug store to keep records of who was buying meth ingredients to the need for more sheriff department horses for patrolling the back woods areas where small meth operations were located.

In 2005, Indiana law put all cold and allergy products containing the active meth ingredients behind the store counters, locked in display cases or under continual video monitoring. Authorities went from being reactive to proactive on all meth-related crimes. The meth problem did not directly affect a lot of us, but it threatened young people and lessened the quality of life for everyone.

On the need for more child protection advocates, the over-burdened caseworker was a well-known story, but paying for the solution was the problem. Mitch talked about it on the road in every corner of the state. In order to make a real difference, the workers were hired and the bottom line was that the money to pay for it would have to be found. And it was.

Although child protection was not an issue covered by pollsters, Mitch insisted on making Indiana's child protection system a top priority. He separated the Department of Child Services (DCS) from the gigantic Family Social Services Agency, added eight hundred more child protection workers, reduced caseloads, and added new protective services for children at risk. After years out of compliance, the court now found Indiana's DCS in compliance. In November of 2007, the Annie E. Casey Foundation recognized Indiana with a national award for the reforms adopted to protect Hoosier children, and received an A+ (97 points out of 100) for its laws regarding child safety information by the Children's Advocacy Institute.

Where more staffing was needed, as with the urgently needed eight hundred new DCS workers, Mitch added state jobs. Child fatalities dropped dramatically and Indiana went from one of the worst to one of the best states for child protection. If they ever make a gubernatorial statue of Mitch, he should have a child in his arms because that is where everything seems to come into focus for him.

Another example of adding, rather than cutting state expenditure, was a necessary 250 state troopers Mitch put on the road. This additional resource helped reduce Indiana's traffic-related deaths, afterward measuring at the lowest level in more than eighty years.

Mitch also pushed the legislature to pass a bill to collect any gambling or lottery winnings from deadbeat dads. At the time Indiana only collected fifty-eight percent of child support, which resulted in $2 billion in delinquencies. In order to motivate deadbeat dads to pull their weight, creative ways were used to get their attention, such as, withholding a hunting or fishing license if a guy was not paying his legal obligation. Nothing motivates some guys like saying they cannot go hunting until they pay their bills.

Mitch said child service improvement and tougher child support enforcement was not only an anti-poverty measure but also, every one percent improvement equaled $6 million for single parents.

Any good fisherman fishes where the fish are. The same is true for any candidate, who should know where his votes or audience reside and where they do not, and then spend his time accordingly. At the outset, crusty insiders faulted our campaign because Mitch spent too much time in rural, low-populated and staunchly Democrat areas at the expense of the old reliable Republican suburban hot bed population centers.

I recall a longtime chamber of commerce war horse who was highly critical of Mitch for spending too much time in one-dot towns and ignoring events, such as annual stuffy coat-and-tie dinners in the capital city, and said this practice would hurt him in the end. The fact was, however, that most people who lived around the capital had come from one of those rural counties, or their parents did, and they were proud Mitch was not flying over their hometown. At the same time he was running up the score in once reliable Democrat territory because he was connecting with them on their issues, whereas his Republican predecessors had written them off.

Mitch even insisted his travel always include visiting one of the most Democrat counties in the nation, Lake County, or *Steel Town* as it became known after the movie. Lake County was in large part a union suburb of Chicago. While we ultimately did not win Lake County which included Gary and East Chicago, going there sent the message that Mitch would leave no community behind and he would root for the whole state, not just attend to particular parts of it that rewarded him.

Early on as he barnstormed the state, Mitch said everyone who shared the goal to make Indiana a better state and sought to help create jobs would be welcome on RV1. We started with a clean slate and gave everyone the benefit of doubt. This welcome mat was even put out to groups with a long history of working against previous Republican nominees for governor, including the union building trades. Instead of ignoring their potential contribution, we sought to find common ground.

Fast forward past his 2004 election, and this developed friendship proved essential in passing one of the most contentious pieces of legislation during the first term, leasing the northern Indiana Toll Road. As mentioned earlier, Major Moves became known as the jobs vote for a generation, equally good to union membership.

No one involved would ever forget the rally at the Indiana State House with union leaders flanking Governor Daniels on stage, speaking out in favor of passing Major Moves, effectively locking in new construction jobs for a decade. Carpenters, operating engineers, electricians, sheet metal workers, and chamber leaders all working together was a surreal sight. Many said they would not have believed it, had they not been there to see it with their own eyes.

Having never held nor sought elective office before made many supporters worried about Mitch's lack of name identification. The opposite proved true. It turned out Hoosiers wanted to give a successful guy out of the business sector the keys to the state and, of course, the name identification came with both the hard work on the trail and effective brand messaging. The once skeptical quickly become your fiercest defenders when you have earned their trust and they begin to see a winner.

Trust in general is not gained through fear or spending $20 million to promote yourself. Trust is earned by doing what you said you would do. The same is true for political trust so do not expect it to be gained by running a commercial with the word "trusted" under your name. And as hard as it is to earn, it is equally easy to lose. It is not as simple as checking your name on the ballot.

Lastly, it is a fact of doing business with those who may not have your future interest in mind that they will prejudge your positions. So, focus on agreeing on shared goals and avoid the past differences and battles.

As one newspaper editorial put it midway through Mitch's first term,

> "Daniels the governor has done pretty much what Daniels the candidate said he would...He promised drastic change, and he delivered. (Daniels) has shaken this state out of its complacency as have few politicians in Indiana history. That opens the door for creative thinking and makes the solution to the state's problems – even seemingly intractable ones – more possible…."(*Fort Wayne News-Sentinel*, September 26, 2006)

If you go, you will meet new friends.

Hard work pays off and brings results.

FOUR

Have Unwavering Dedication to Your Beliefs

THROUGH UNWAVERING DEDICATION TO your core beliefs you will be afforded tomorrow's political capital to spend on future projects. The political account balance of your accumulated capital will provide you strength and thus frame you as a strong or weak leader. Obviously, this comes at a price, as tough times call for tough decisions, and you will be both strategically and ignorantly attacked by your opponents for your stands. On such days, it is not unusual for the candidate to feel as though all day long he or she has been catching arrows barehanded and dancing to dodge bullets.

Incumbents and challengers running for office have records and pasts. Everything seems to be fair game as your opponent explores and seeks to score points with the public. Expect it and prepare for it; after all, there is no crying in baseball or politics. The fastest way to watch your closest friends scatter for the hills and go silent on your proposals is for you to start second guessing one of your core beliefs out of perceived political expediency. In governing, trying to please everyone all the time, as they say, is the surest way to be liked temporarily but accomplish nothing that stands the test of time. It takes courage to follow through when the vocal minority's incoming fire starts to rain down on your parade.

To be honest, it is hard to keep the team together, all oaring in the same direction when you actually start doing things and breaking eggs to make all those omelets. I recall traditionally supportive state legislators getting weak-kneed after Mitch pushed for leasing Indiana's money-losing Toll Road, again; supporting daylight saving time; closing small town Bureau of Motor Vehicle branches that were providing inefficient service, or even simply cutting the growth of government spending to balance the budget.

It is one thing to talk about limiting the size and scope of government, but wait until you start doing it; even once dyed-in-the wool Republicans get soft on losing the gift of giving government goodies to expectant voters.

In the first couple years of his first term, some polling released on the governor, rated him below forty percent in the approval category. The biggest newspaper in the state, *The Indianapolis Star*, published commentary about how unpopular the then first-term governor was. There was even chatter the governor was a sure bet to be a one-termer, and in fact, it was speculated he might not even run for a second term because he was taking on too much too fast to ever realize being reelected. Some said he was trying to build Rome in a day. The consensus was "if" he ran for reelection, there was no way he would win, and that was coming from our friends.

And our opponents tried to brand the governor as a bully. I would be less than truthful not to admit that many of us asked ourselves, "Did we do too much, too fast?" But the political insider's echo chamber is always smaller than insiders think and if you are not pushing yourself to the limit, you probably are not ever going to reach your potential.

It is here you must reconnect to the passion that drove you to run in the first place. Remind yourself of your short- and long-term goals and your vision, rather than being consumed by thoughts of how to get elected. Voters will be reassured that you mean what you say and will not be held prisoner by political pundits, polling, special interest groups, or a few bad headlines. You will need to be flexible enough to allow your plans to evolve and, through cooperation, improve upon them. But you should also literally make a list of what you will not compromise on and keep it in the top drawer of your desk.

Churchill was right when he said, *"Never, never, never give up,"* and things worth fighting for, such as our freedom and the future, fall into the "never give up" category. If at first you do not succeed doesn't mean the defenders of the status quo win. Even against constant resistance, you must never quit on your customers and ultimately they will not quit on you.

Mitch always said, "We will make mistakes, but they will be mistakes of commission (action), not omission (inaction)," and that we would learn from and not repeat them. In fact, if you are going to fail, fail fast and get on with it. That might sound obvious, but not in politics. The Daniels Administration's posture was always to have one foot forward, playing the ball, always willing, not fearing, to make mistakes. In fact, Mitch expected those around him to try new things by taking calculated risks in quest of new results.

It has been said, *"Without pressure, there are no diamonds,"* so accepting the pressure and risk of failure that go along with leading gives your team a much longer leash on which to venture out to uncharted territory. In today's environment, there is a good chance the same old recycled solutions are not going to solve modern problems, rhetoric aside, of course.

And just when we thought it could not get any hotter in the kitchen during his first term, instead of letting up as he was going into a reelection campaign, when most frontrunners are advised to play it safe, Mitch turned it up a few more degrees and warned citizens to *"Buckle up!"* More was on its way. In effect, *"Damn the torpedoes, full steam ahead!"*

Mitch started talking seriously about reforming education and more about updating the Civil War-era structured local governments while his opponent spent time and money rehashing and stoking yesteryears' tired issues.

In Indiana, Mitch not only redefined how to run for governor but then more importantly, how to govern. His vigorous and fresh style proved the old line "good policy makes good politics" and showed that the big problems we face can be solved. So it is no wonder voters in Indiana became less cynical and believed the state was on the right track going forward.

Keep in mind, during the early years, the Democrat speaker of the house actually said Mitch was "the most unpopular governor ever elected in Indiana." Fast forward two years when Mitch won reelection, receiving more votes than anyone who had ever run for office in Indiana. In fact, that made him the most popular governor in state history, judging by the actual votes, but who is counting?

While many believed destiny played a factor in Mitch being elected in 2004, many came to believe that his bold leadership was needed even more the following four years. It was not unusual to hear even those who did not vote for Mitch confess that they were glad he was leading the state during the turbulent national recession. Tough times demand tough leadership.

Do not be politically afraid to take on hot button issues in pursuit of making government work.

Yes, change is hard. If it were easy, many changes would have already been made. And the harder the change, the harder the champions of the status quo will push back against the forces of progress. You will be required to maintain a disciplined focus on your priorities and to compartmentalize vicious personal attacks on your integrity.

One tactic against change is the opponent who tries to demoralize you and thus extinguish your ideas. Those who have the ability to smile and shut out the self-serving nay-sayers will rise above the petty politics. Easier said than done during the heat of battle, but try not to let illogical, inaccurate, or demeaning remarks get your goat.

Another after-years-of-trying story was the saga of how we finally came to observe daylight saving time (DST). DST had been debated for decades in Indiana. No one ever claimed it would be the cure-all in and of itself, but there was no dispute that it would eliminate unending time-related business confusion. Half the year part of the state recognized one time zone while other regions recognized another. To complicate the issue, each spring and fall clocks had to be turned an hour forward or back, depending on the county where you lived. It was common in one county to see two clocks on the kitchen wall because just across the county line, the time zone was different.

Opponents of DST said school children would get hit by busses in the dark, cows would quit giving milk, and businesses would go under. Of course none of that happened, but what did happen was companies, such as FedEx, added hundreds of jobs at the Indianapolis Airport, and truckers cheered because the chaos of the state's time zone being out of sync was once and for all settled, ushering Indiana into the twenty-first century.

You would think a state that sells itself as the crossroads of America would understand time management had to be an asset, not a liability, in order for the state to grow. After Mitch pushed and passed DST, past opponents started to openly admit that if you wanted something difficult resolved, you needed Mitch's support.

Recall, for decades Indiana had failed to generate enough funding to maintain roads and bridges or pay for promised future projects. The roads and bridges remained simply blueprints in a drawer. When Mitch assumed office, he inherited those blueprints and decided to try a creative new approach. Leasing the only state toll road to the highest bidder through the $3.85 billion Major Moves program was certainly as controversial as passing DST.

I recall days when opponents warned us that leasing a state asset to a foreign company for years on end would be as smart as leasing something to Germany before Hitler took control. China bashing was favored by the left. For folks who considered themselves the tolerant class, stoking xenophobia became *en vogue* and their line of attack. Never mind that we would be using other people's money to pay off our original toll road debt in addition to building hundreds of new projects. The opponents of private sector management still feared government jobs would be at risk. While we negotiated the lease, we made it clear that the private company would first interview all the state employees who had worked on the toll road and offer them jobs first if they wanted the work. Most did. They simply went to work for a private company, not the state.

Another example of sticking to your guns in the heat of battle occurred as the 2009 legislative session came within hours of ending with no budget agreement in sight. So Mitch set his sights on an obvious tool – the Bureau of Motor Vehicles. Everyone had his or her own old horror story about waiting hours on end at a local branch. Mitch used to joke about "taking a boxed lunch and a copy of *War and Peace*, hoping you did not finish both by the time your business was completed." But that was the bureau of the past. After restoring the Bureau, everyone raved about the efficiency of their local branch.

So, at the last hour, with the budget still in limbo, the Indiana Bureau of Motor Vehicles (BMV) closed all its branches indefinitely and put up signs that read: "All license branches are CLOSED because the Indiana General Assembly failed to approve a state budget. Customers with appointments will need to reschedule after we reopen. We apologize for the inconvenience. Contact your legislator at 1-800-382-9842."

Opponents of the proposed balanced budget caved immediately and passed the legislation, fearing the public's wrath. This creative strategy produced a political two-fer. During the State House of Representative races the next year, ads ran targeting representatives who had wanted to spend a billion dollars we did not have and would have busted the balanced budget. This reminder to the public in part helped convert the Republican minority to the sixty-seat Republican majority that would go on to pass the historic education reforms of 2011.

Now anyone in Indiana can check license branch location wait times from his computer. With ninety-eight percent of all BMV transactions now available online or at an automobile dealer or AAA Hoosier Motor Club office, there is little reason to visit a branch in person, which reduces the wait time if you do physically go to a branch as in the old days. You can also make an appointment if necessary, just like getting a haircut. In the end, new branches were opened and old branches closed where traffic did not warrant the expenditure.

With an under fourteen-minute average total visit at any time at any statewide BMV branch and an overall satisfaction rate of ninety-seven percent, it is no surprise that in July 2008, and again in 2010, the Indiana Bureau of Motor Vehicles received the International Customer Service Excellence Award for the best state bureau in the country.

Every state agency had to go through its budget and make cut after painful cut. In the end, almost every agency eliminated twenty percent of its costs. Many agency heads did not believe it was possible but, barring jeopardizing public safety, everyone was expected to bite the bullet. Employees would have to understand that to get out of the woods, there would be no automatic pay raises. And Mitch said, "You'll never know how much government you'll never miss."

Keep in mind, voters will understand, accept, and even reward candidates whom they perceive to mean what they say and say what they mean, even if they do not agree one hundred percent of the time. If you tell taxpayers you will balance the books, they will understand when you have to make tough choices to get there.

Voters will understand and cut you some slack but do not expect your opponents to; especially when they are the proponents of spending more than you have. Our loyal opposition was obsessed with the idea that the only reason Mitch kept cutting and wanted to protect a healthy savings account was because he was running for President. In reality, the plot was not that tricky. Asked how he balanced our budgets through difficult times, Mitch always said, "Prepare to be dazzled; we spent less than we took in."

In a warning to all, Mitch penned the following on this topic in *The Wall Street Journal Op Ed*, September 3, 2009:

"Sadly, the political impulse to protect government largess leads many states to aggravate their dilemma. Already more than half have raised taxes, often on businesses, serving only to chase them and their tax payments away and into the open arms of states like Indiana. Our traffic flow of interested investors is as heavy as it was in 2007. Since January we have welcomed the consolidation of more than 30 firms that closed up shop elsewhere and chose us as the low-cost, enterprise-friendly environment among their current locations.

"Indiana was near bankruptcy five years ago but is relatively solvent today because we have spent the intervening years making hard choices. We have reformed state procurement, contracted out some jobs, cut costs, and relentlessly scrutinized expenditures in pushing for annual improvement in departments large and small. We've also reduced the number of state employees by some 5,000 from the 2004 level.

"In contrast to the national pattern, our per capita state spending has cut, on average, 1.4% each of the past five years. Indiana is now the sixth thriftiest state by this measure. And if we Hoosiers are realizing that we need to re-examine what we can afford to have our government do, what must they be thinking in Albany, Lansing or Trenton?"

If at first you do not succeed, do not quit.
Be willing to fail (temporarily).

If you have never failed, you have never pushed it and, worse, never learned from failure. Failure provides you the opportunity for lessons that may not present themselves any other way. During his first term Mitch proposed building the Illiana Expressway project to ease traffic congestion around Chicago and to encourage economic development in the region. Although Mitch believed it was needed, there were not enough champions outside his Administration and stakeholders to push it through. He said that if local citizens could make the case and gain the necessary public support, he would be their biggest cheerleader.

That is exactly what happened a few years later. In his second term, Mitch once again found union allies in the Operating Engineers, supporters among local economic development officials, and a new ally in Illinois Governor Pat Quinn (D), who all saw the wisdom in building the expressway. Quinn and Daniels signed a memorandum of understanding which put in motion the necessary studies, consideration of potential routes and allowed collaboration with private contractors to build and manage the new road. Working across the aisle with another governor in Kentucky attracted the notice of Bellarmine University for their bipartisan work to build bridges over the Ohio River that had been talked about for forty years.

Mitch also proposed building another loop around Indianapolis outside I-465, or a connector, to accommodate through-traffic, say from Louisville to Chicago, and alleviate local Indianapolis area congestion on existing interstates and highways.

He described the potential project in his 2007 *State of the State Address* as "linking four interstates at six job-magnetic hubs, could give a large swath of our state another big edge on the competition. Local leaders all around both these potential routes have reacted with enthusiasm to their potential to invigorate their economies."

But this project was ahead of its time and went nowhere. A logical next step for a future governor will occur when future traffic congestion leads to crisis and no other alternatives are available.

You cannot know what folks are thinking unless you are listening.

Create harmony wherever you go.

FIVE

Timing, Tempo and Tone

MOST EXPERIENCED CAMPAIGNERS WILL tell you the three most important things in a campaign are money, money, and money. It is true, money is essential, but there are other not so obvious factors that equally affect the outcome, such as the three T's of any successful message: timing, tempo and tone. Successful campaigns usually have a subtle synergy among these three elements.

Timing is not only important in taking the temperature or the mood of the electorate; it is also critical to know when to roll out policy items for public consumption. Each year is different from both the previous year and the one to follow. First, survey and know the market landscape; then determine if your project or ideas have a resonating appeal. It has been said, "Pioneers take the arrows, settlers take the land," so avoid premature ideas and pursue only those you are passionate about and willing to work hard for to make a reality.

Second, because people are busy or preoccupied, they have a limited capacity to process complex messages from candidates and elected officials alike. By promising too much, you may be left with a confused electorate and accomplish nothing. Exaggerating or promising the moon makes your to-do list less credible, not more. How your proposals make a taxpayer's life easier will determine what they listen to and like. Time and issue management go hand-in-glove.

If your timing is right, *carpe diem.* You are never too old or too young if your ideas gain traction. Once you have determined you are moving forward, it is time to think about the tempo of your policy rollouts. The tempo is a layer many miss, but every good public relations campaign has a rhythm or cadence to it. Voters will begin to view the campaign as a source of thoughtful ideas. Remember, it is better to be known as a well of information rather than of a fountain that sprays at the start but fizzles out over time.

Whether they realize it or not, taxpayers expect the public servant they hire to keep up a certain pace but not to exceed their ability to follow. If you get too far ahead of them, they may begin to think you are working for yourself, not them. Likewise, if you have a reputation for being a hard charger with an appetite for reform and change, be consistent and do not let up after victories or defeats. Otherwise, folks will start to believe you represent only a slogan.

Lastly, woven into the fabric with timing and tempo is the overall tone your customers will hear and recognize as your brand. It is not just what you say; it is how you say it. If you campaign that you will be tough on crime, you had better reduce crime and be able to prove it. If you campaign that you will create a better economic development environment, you had better be able to point to job creation. Campaign on hope and change and the next time around voters should be even more hopeful because of the change you brought about.

Whether you are a challenger or an incumbent, your tone and purpose should be the same. As a challenger, it is not only permissible to compare your approach to solving problems and expectations to your opponent's; it is necessary. You must say what you mean and mean what you say. The key is to realize that going negative on your opponent is not the same as comparing your records. Make the most of your opportunities to showcase your plan.

I have heard many people claim Governor Mitch Daniels never went negative because he did not have to. True, but that is because he seized the high ground and rejected any temptation to lurch toward gutter politics. It takes discipline not to, but no one has to go negative. A simple rule is to manage and promote the substance of your ideas and the politics will take care of themselves. Do not rely on DC talking points to persuade the American public, but instead spend time figuring out how to share the compelling reasons why your ideas will carry the day.

Upon first taking office, Mitch set out to get Indiana's fiscal house in order, pay off all debts to local governments and schools, honestly balance the budget, and improve state government services. Once the government's foundation is on solid fiscal ground, then you can look to responsible tax cuts and other government reforms that grow the economy and enhance revenue.

On his second day, Governor Daniels issued an executive order ending the collective bargaining for state government unions that previous administrations had put in place. The practice of collective bargaining in a practical sense prevented state agencies from making big changes, but many joked that state employees could not even move tables and chairs around in the government center cafeteria without first asking the union's permission.

Today, state government can be much more nimble and cost-effective. Indiana now pays state employees based on performance, has improved state service and operates at the same staffing level as it did in 1975, before collective bargaining. While other states were ballooning their government rolls, Indiana had the ability to right-size.

Elections make a difference, and the threat of a government union revolution proved to be a paper tiger. Over ninety percent of former state employee union dues-paying members voluntarily opted out of the government union umbrella. Even hard hat union members did not get over-exercised about the new arrangement for state employees. Some Union members just wanted a voice, not a big brother.

As it turned out, former members wanted to give themselves a pay raise more than they wanted to pay their union bosses. Safety conditions were handled by OSHA, and the federal government appeared to provide all the discrimination protection an offended employee may seek. After Mitch ended collective bargaining, fewer than fifty people showed up at Indiana AFSCME rallies whereas in 1995, union members filled the state house second floor.

Taxpayers want their government to work and produce results. What they do not expect is gridlock. Any time you can bridge the party divide and bring competitors together, the public overwhelmingly approves.

For example, just as soon as it was financially feasible, Mitch decided it was time to fulfill a longtime Democratic dream of expanding full-day kindergarten (FDK), and he explained it in terms moms and dads of any political persuasion could relate to:

"The main reason I pressed for an immediate return to balanced budgets was so that we could again have the funds to strengthen public education. I hope this Assembly will provide at least a quarter billion dollars in new funding for the system as it stands today.

"But the time has come to augment that system, to make certain that every Indiana child arrives at first grade ready for the tasks ahead. After years of study, debate, and failed attempts, let's make an irrevocable commitment to full-day kindergarten for every family that wants it, starting with our lowest-income children, starting when school opens this fall.

"Cooperation requires giving credit where it is due. This proposal came first from members of the Democratic Party. It was your governors, and many of your legislators still serving, who first advanced and attempted this step. You were right.

"After listening for months to educators, parents, and all the experts I could find, I have laid out one possible approach that tries to blend the many disparate views on this topic. To both sides of this chamber, I say, modify that proposal, refine and improve it as I know you can, but let's act now, together, to make full-day kindergarten real in 2007." (*2007 State of the State Address*)

Throughout his first term, Mitch often cited Indiana's lack of educational improvement as his biggest regret. While he expanded full-day kindergarten and passed a law that allowed Indiana's attorney general to represent teachers so they did not have to rely soley on the teachers' union, much work still needed to be done on the education front in order to really move the needle.

Indiana ranked fiftieth nationwide in the percentage of all K-12 public school employees who were teachers, but Hoosiers spent fourteen percent more of their income on K-12 schools than the US average. For example, Indiana spent more on the construction of schools than forty-eight other states. Over fifty-six percent of the state's budget was devoted to K-12 spending which was also more than any other state and yet, test scores and the rates of high school graduation did not reflect this investment.

Part of the explanation was the fact that the expenditure did not make it into the classroom. The taxpayers' money was being spent outside the classroom on administrative staff, superintendants' and principals' offices, transportation and support staff.

An average Indiana teacher was making more than the average Hoosier worker (48K to 39K) for working nine-to-ten months of the year. The disparity increased when benefits were considered in the equation. The average worker's income went down during the recession while teachers' salaries went up every year because of one factor: the strong teachers' union in Indiana. The union was the authority that represented and defended all teachers, not differentiating between teachers who inspired and motivated kids and teachers who were ineffectual or even detrimental to their students' learning.

First, it was a political fact that what was needed was a State House, Senate, and Governor who were willing to do battle with the professional education union bureaucracy. In the election of 2010, Republicans went from the State House minority to the majority overnight. The impossible seemed, for the first time, possible, but it still would not be easy. Without the majority in friendly, open-minded hands, education reform would have suffered the same fate as many local government reform bills and been killed in committee before even being granted a hearing.

Armed with these energetic majorities, Mitch struck when the iron was hot and passed four major education reform that:

- expanded school choice options
- increased school accountability standards
- improved teacher quality standards
- limited the stranglehold collective bargaining had over local schools

In addition to the four major reforms, he passed another interesting idea for high school students to consider. For squared-away high school juniors who had already completed all the necessary graduation requirements, the state agreed to apply the amount that would have been used to pay for a student's senior year to his or her first year of in-state college tuition. As a result, Indiana was seen as a national leader when it came to education reform, when one election before, upgrading education seemed destined to remain the biggest regret.

Understanding who your wish list allies are is important. As the CEO, never lose sight of the public's appetite for reform, but understand that each of your legislative friends represents a wide political spectrum and each has personal reasons for serving. In the first two years of office, Mitch was able to eliminate antiquated programs, install an inspector general, pass the contentious observation of daylight saving time, and lease Indiana's only toll road.

Two years later, working with a member of the opposite party from the famous Lake County, Indiana he passed a market-based healthcare program for thousands who did not have insurance, in addition to expanding full-day kindergarten.

Big reform followed big reform, and the culture of complacency was overturned in favor of aggressive play. No longer would Indiana be known as cornfields or a place to refuel the jet while en route from New York to LA. Hoosiers began to ask, "What's next?" and "How do we expand our lead?" The same things we expect from our favorite sports teams.

And lastly, you could quickly assess the tone Mitch set from day one of the first campaign. His tone or voice was always inspirational and confident. On election night 2004, Mitch said it best when he told the packed room:

> "Citizens of Indiana, my fellow Hoosiers, you have favored me tonight with the sixth biggest moment of my life. There's a five-way tie for first – those being the days when each of the Daniels women came on the scene. Won't you say "hi" to Cheri and the girls?
>
> "Our future partners, Becky's and mine in state government. To the members of the next Indiana General Assembly, congratulations on your election. Buckle up.
>
> "We have important work to do, big changes to bring, courageous decisions to make. Working together, across all boundaries of parties and geography and philosophy, we must tackle Indiana's problems and achieve Indiana's potential in a way that brings honor to our state and progress to all 6.1 million of our fellow citizens.
>
> "So tonight, for one night, I say let 'er rip! But when the music stops and the fun is finally over, drive home safely. Get a good rest. Get your courage up and your game face on because the real work starts tomorrow."

And, when issuing a call to arms, the message must be clear, welcoming and appealing to anyone wishing to aim higher. First inaugurals by their very nature hold special places throughout history. The emotion of coming off the first victory can be felt when reading former governors' or presidents' first inaugural addresses. The same is true for Mitch when he framed his call around a topic near and dear to Hoosier hearts…raising a barn. He said,

> "It's time to raise a new barn in Indiana, a new, stronger structure to house new tools and to make possible far richer future harvests. We will need the whole community to show up. As a government, we will do all that is possible to clear the path for new jobs and investment, but our businesses must take the risks from which alone new wealth comes.
>
> "We will spend the tax dollars of Hoosiers whenever possible inside our state, but our corporations must do likewise, and our universities must also use every opportunity to help the neighbors whose tax dollars support them.
>
> "Our utilities, granted special privileges by the nature of their product, must commit themselves to helping us attract new business. Those to whom life in Indiana has been the most kind must be willing to give back in accordance with their good fortune. And every interest group, of every kind and cause, must resolve to demand a little less, relent a little more often, if we are going to get the new barn up with the limited resources on hand.
>
> "Let's nobody sit home. Every parent who checks homework or reads to a child is lifting a bigger hammer than they may realize. Every person who volunteers at a free clinic, a food bank, a nursing home is putting a

plank in place. Every young person who studies a little harder or signs up for a tougher course is driving a nail. Every citizen who stops smoking, or loses a few pounds, or starts managing his chronic disease with real diligence, is caulking a crack for the benefit of us all.

"The young people of Indiana are watching us today, whether their classroom is tuned in or not. I know, from having met thousands of them, in their schools, at their games, and on the streets of their towns, that they love this state, and overwhelmingly they hope to make it their home as adults. Over and over, they have told me in identical words: "I want to stay, but…"

"They are watching now to see whether we who are already adults will behave like it. Whether we have a fraction of the fortitude our ancestors had in such abundance. Whether we will rebuild the barn, pay our debts, and leave the family business strong, so that they can carry it on and pay the bills when their turn comes.

"When we meet again in eight days, I will lay out a design for our new community rebuilding project. I will suggest the roles each of us can undertake. I will urge that our purpose be bold, that if we err, we err on the side of action, of movement, of experiment. And that our aim be high. It's been said that every great achievement was first a dream; cathedrals are not brought into being by skeptics.

"Neither are great barns." (*First Inaugural Address*, January 10, 2005)

Hard to top that connection, but in a span of just two months, Mitch delivered his election night victory speech, his first inaugural address and closed with his first state of the state address by respectfully reaching out to allies and adversaries alike, calling for a broad partnership in the progress that lay ahead. He said,

"This is a great moment for everyone in this chamber. How lucky we are to have been chosen at this particular time. Some of you must have had the same experience as I these last two months. In every conversation, it seems, the other party sooner or later uses the word 'excited.' Our fellow citizens are excited because, knowing full well the state of our state, they believe fervently that Indiana can be a better place. Who could ask for more as a public servant than to serve at a time of large issues, true crises, and high expectations that things can be vastly different?" *(2005 State of the State Address)*

In his *2006 State of the State Address*, he kept aiming higher.

"As an utterly forgettable young infielder, I heard far too often the coaches shout "Daniels, don't let the ball play you." They meant to get off your heels and move forward, advance on ground balls and field them before it was too late. If you mishandled the first attempt, there would still be time to try again and throw the runner out at first.

"Indiana is no longer on its heels, waiting while our problems bounce past us or through our legs. Even though the inning is still an early one, we are moving forward against our challenges. We are playing the ball."

Even his critical comments about others tended to be metaphorical rather than insulting, and never personal. For instance, during his first campaign, he said, "Every 16 years the garden needs weeding," rather than the tired "they must go" mantra we hear all too often. Mitch said, "We haven't been governed by bad people, but we have been governed badly."

And after a memorable first term, full of hard work and accomplishment, he articulated just what it meant to get our fiscal house in order and arrange a state government in a way that best served its investors. In his *Second Inaugural Address*, January 12, 2009, he said:

"A moment of worldwide economic anxiety may seem an odd time for words of hope and visions of greatness. All are aware that the days immediately before us will not be traversed without much difficulty.

"But we must believe, and resolve to see, that these present troubles are but a frost in April, a brief chill before the full flowering of the greener Indiana to come.

"Not even the cold realities of a wintry world economy can obscure the signs of spring in our state. Out of economic erosion and indistinction, Indiana now excels in every assessment of appeal to new plantings of future jobs and prosperity. A blossoming culture of enterprise foretells the coming vigor of a youthful economy that regenerates new sprouts faster than its trusted old branches decay and fall away.

"Best of all, a new mentality has taken root, a new boldness born of risks successfully run and change successfully delivered. In overwhelming numbers, Hoosiers have declared that we are unafraid to lead, to try the new before others do, and that we like the results of doing so.

"No more will historians write that we are backward and out of step. That we are, at best, 'gradualists' who prefer to keep to "the more secure edge of the river.

"The Indiana they depicted would never have led the nation in capturing international investment, cutting and reforming property taxes, or bringing peace of mind to those without health insurance. That Indiana would never have devised a way to build public infrastructure in record amounts without a penny of taxes or borrowing, or to liberate the new infrastructure of fiber and frequency in a nationally innovative way.

"In dramatic contradiction of old stereotypes, Hoosiers have announced emphatically to a world that belongs to the creative and nimble, where fortune truly favors the bold, that we not only accept change but are prepared to lead it, and invite the rest of America to follow us."

And followed it up in his *2009 State of the State Address,* saying:

"I awake every day glad for many reasons that I am a Hoosier. And though we meet tonight in an hour of great stress, we have cause if not for gladness then at least for relief, that it is in Indiana we are meeting. For, thanks in large part to the people here assembled, we can speak tonight of challenge, but not crisis; issues, but not emergencies. We will examine the state of our state soberly, but with satisfaction in the knowledge that here the people's business has been handled better than in so many other places. We will speak realistically, but positively, recognizing that in predicament there is opportunity, and in tough times the possibility to separate from the pack and emerge stronger than before.

"No assignment will test us all more than our most basic one, the proper stewardship of the people's money. Global trends set in motion far from here have severely reduced the revenue available for public purposes in the indefinite future. So be it. Thanks to the prudence, and the courage, of people present, Indiana faces this recession in far different shape than it did on past occasions, and far different condition than our sister states. People on this floor crafted with us consecutively two of the tightest budgets in state history. People in those balconies have managed government with businesslike care for every tax dollar. Together, you not only brought our state out of bankruptcy, you placed it in strong condition to weather the difficulties ahead. You merit the thanks of those who sent you here for a job well done.

"We must apply the principles that have served us so well to the tasks now before us. I have submitted to you a budget proposal that meets the test of honest balance, by spending no more than it takes in. It does so despite the daunting projection that revenues will still be lower two years from now than we were told to expect in this fiscal year."

The first campaign commercial out of the gate in 2008 was Mitch saying to the camera:

"I don't expect anybody to agree with all of them. There are too many (changes)."

I heard more people repeat that line and personally identify with it than any other line in any other commercial. But as much as that line looked back, setting the stage, Mitch always focused on the future, never bragging about the past accomplishments. It is key to look forward, not back as Jimmy Buffett instructs when he sings, "Don't need to look over my shoulder to see what I'm after."

By the way, if you speak to the future, the youth will not only listen, they will hear you. If you talk about FDR or Ronald Reagan for that matter, as prominent as they were, you might as well be talking about Millard Fillmore or Franklin Pierce.

Remember, when you base your campaign on the belief that ideas matter, you cannot be the candidate from the Party of NO or Obstruction. Being negative usually yields negative results. When Mitch's opponents hurled untrue accusations about the Indianapolis Power and Light Company stock he sold, many advised him to hit back hard. I am convinced resisting that advice was key to taking the high ground we occupied afterward. Mitch dedicated himself to running three positive campaigns (one primary followed by two generals) that Hoosiers could be proud of, and he did it the old-fashioned way. He earned it.

Lastly, keep your word. Write down your goals and share them strategically every chance you get. Again, make sure your message is clear and easy to repeat. Our Road Maps served this purpose brilliantly. After the message is established, synchronize all other campaign communication pipelines, such as direct mail, radio, newspaper, and television advertising to echo your themes.

When you do, you will find that sometimes even critics appreciate the positive approach. For example, former Democratic Indiana State Senator Connie Sipes said after a State of the State Address: "I think the Governor was of course upbeat -

complimentary of the legislators, complimentary of the staff. He was proud of the state, and we share that," Sipes said. "I respected his tone tonight."

There will be slip-ups. When they occur, own up to them. Even Mitch made a couple mistakes he had to admit. One occurred after the Indiana Court of Appeals ruled that the Indiana Voter ID law violated the Indiana Constitution because the Court believed it "regulates voters in a manner that is not uniform and impartial." Well, of course nothing could have been further from the truth and it did not take a law degree to know so.

Governor Daniels reacted to the Court's decision by calling the ruling "transparently partisan" and went on to say, "It's a preposterous decision, an extreme decision and came in this case from a judge who's been reversed before and I expect it to happen again." He even called it an "act of judicial arrogance."

In the end, the governor was right and Indiana's Court of Appeals decision was overturned, but that did not change the fact the governor could have moderated his personal charge and voiced a more constructive perspective.

Even an unthinking phrase can be turned on you if it sensationalizes a description of someone or something. The Speaker of the House from the opposing party seemed to have as a priority, making the governor look ineffective by staging a surprise walkout in an attempt to defeat Mitch's first session legislative items. Tired of this tactic, Mitch declared the speaker had "car bombed" one of his early legislative agendas, and from there, the issue took on a life of its own.

The speaker quickly played victim and the entire exchange became a sideshow, serving his strategy. Any time lost on damage control by the governor was seen as a good thing from the loyal opposition's perspective. What did we learn? Be prepared for the opposition to use your own words against you, so choose your words carefully. Or as my grandmother used to say, "Keep your words sweet, for you may have to eat them."

The best collection of stories illustrating the tone of a campaign can be found in Mitch's first book, *Notes from the Road*. In his book you can find examples of the places he traveled in RV1, listened and heard, connected with folks, laughed, learned, spread his message, and ate and slept on his journey to the governor's office.

A good leader makes sure the train runs on time.

Indiana farmers host Mitch at breakfast to discuss how to increase agricultural production and the adverse impact of politically-motivated regulations on the family farm.

SIX

Sell, Sell, Sell...
Then Sell Again

ASK ANY LEADER WHO has failed to persuade constituents to help achieve an important goal, "What would you do differently?" Odds are the response would be, "I would sell more."

Selling public policy is like playing volleyball and requires at minimum three actions:

1. Set
2. Spike
3. Follow through

For an idea to get traction, you must be determined but do not act in haste. Carefully plan who will be with you at your announcement kickoff and how many stops around the state will be required to burn your message. If you think checking five media market boxes or touching down on four tarmacs will cut it, think again. Cover the big media markets, but also complement them with smaller markets, the ones without television stations. Today's technology connects news stories in a small town to both coasts with a push of the send button. With instant messaging and cell phone cameras, videos become commercials that go viral within seconds.

The staged press conference behind a borrowed, beat-up oak wood podium in front of four reporters on folding chairs isn't maximum coverage. Visit a local high school and talk to a full auditorium. Take questions from students about your topic as well as anything else on their minds. The photos and B-roll will be lively, an eyeful. Meet separately with the media gaggle so reporters do not interrupt the conversation flow.

Attend high school and college football and basketball games and track meets. Both the perception and reality that you are accessible will discredit any attack from your opponent who tries to claim you are insulated from the working peoples' troubles or are afraid of public interaction. Everyday folks will appreciate the fact that even if you do not visit their high school, you might one day.

Stop in the local watering hole and have breakfast where the Liars' Club meets. Every town has a diner where the retired school superintendent, former sheriff, mayor and hardware store owner meet for coffee, biscuits and gravy, and eggs. You can learn more about what a community thinks in an hour at the Main Street Café than you might the rest of the day. You eat what they eat, you hear what they hear and they tell you what they think.

A good two or three day trip with a couple overnights, a high school basketball game, a town hall meeting, breakfast and lunch on the square, and a few in-studio local radio interviews around the state will lay the necessary foundation from which to hone your message. Add email updates and Facebook video clips to your data base of supporters, fans or customers and you have come out of the gate strong.

Making yourself accessible demonstrates that you are open to challenge and welcome input, which some will find as important as the idea itself. On the contrary if you never leave your office, folks begin to think you are crafting back-room deals and are beholden to a small number of influential characters. If you start to project a bunker mentality the next time you hit the road, your stops will appear more like stunts. Keep a regular travel log and you will not lose the valuable insights, perceptions, anecdotes, and quotes you picked up on the fly.

While you start with citizens, you must also reach leaders, namely legislators, who can determine the ultimate success or failure of an idea. When you meet with the press, inviting a legislator who has fought for an issue for years will put your views inside that person's caucus when you are not there to advocate. Legislators can become your surrogates and are better equipped to whip up support if they have been exposed to the same line of questioning you have. It also helps the legislator's status and cements him or her to you.

If you want to build more nature trails, have the outdoor enthusiasts stand with you and publicly recognize them. If you want to create jobs, ask small business owners to come with you. Bring in road builders if you want to build more roads. Speak Spanish, if you can, when you are interviewed about education on Spanish radio or television. Or bring your own interpreter if you cannot. It can be dangerous to rely on others goodwill in translations

Always remember, a picture is worth a thousand words, literally, and the picture is burned instantly if the viewer recognizes a local person with you. Most of the time, viewers hear "blah blah blah" when politicians speak on the six or eleven o'clock news. Have hooks that reach into the community.

Always know your audiences. If you are speaking at a university commencement, be original and seek to inspire with a message that provokes thought beyond "do your part to make this world a better place." Mitch delivered some controversial and provocative thoughts during commencement speeches over the years. At Butler University, in May of 2009, Mitch told the graduates, as faculty and proud parents looked on:

"Which leads me to congratulate you in advance. As a generation, you are off to an excellent start. You have taken the first savvy step on the road to distinction, which is to follow a weak act. I wish I could claim otherwise, but we Baby Boomers are likely to be remembered by history for our numbers, and little else, at least little else that is admirable.

"We Boomers were the children that the Second World War was fought for. Parents who had endured both war and the Great Depression devoted themselves sacrificially to ensuring us a better life than they had. We were pampered in ways no children in human history would recognize. With minor exceptions, we have lived in blissfully fortunate times. The numbers of us who perished in plagues, in famine, or in combat were tiny in comparison to previous generations of Americans, to say nothing of humanity elsewhere.

"All our lives, it's been all about us. We were the 'Me Generation.' We wore T-shirts that said, 'If it feels good, do it.' The year of my high school commencement, a hit song featured the immortal lyric 'Sha-la-la-la-la-la, live for today.' As a group, we have been self-centered, self-absorbed, self-indulgent, and all too often just plain selfish. Our current Baby Boomer President has written two eloquent, erudite books, both about himself.

"As a generation, we did tend to live for today. We have spent more and saved less than any previous Americans. Year after year, regardless which party we picked to lead the country, we ran up deficits that have multiplied the debt you and your children will be paying off your entire working lives. Far more burdensome to you mathematically, we voted ourselves increasing levels of Social Security pensions and Medicare healthcare benefits, but never summoned the political maturity to put those programs on anything resembling a sound actuarial footing.

"In sum, our parents scrimped and saved to provide us a better living standard than theirs; we borrowed and splurged and will leave you a staggering pile of bills to pay. It's been a blast; good luck cleaning up after us."

Believe me when I tell you the students smiled and cheered while many of the faculty sneered. More often than not, the ideas that require the most selling are the hard ones; otherwise they would have been accomplished a long time ago. There will be easy fights, like cracking down on deadbeat dads or cracking down on meth. Who is not for those, except for the felons themselves? But most initiatives will require a clear message to educate folks on the problem and a commitment to say it a hundred times. And still, if at first you do not succeed, you must try, try again. As many times as it takes.

At times, you may feel alone on your journey to right-size government or cut annual spending growth, and temporarily, you might be. It is easy to say you are for limited government, but harder to lead the effort to reduce the size and scope of it. But if you put in your road time, you will gain the support of the man on the street. Soon, others will gravitate to your vision, so be patient and persistent in the beginning and you will run into like-minded people. Encourage and enlist them to help spread the word. Having partners will force your opponents to focus on multiple targets, not just you and your big idea.

The day will come when the facts prevail. It may not be today, this year or in five years, but they will. That is why you must always be able to personalize the reasons why you are promoting a particular change. How will it change someone's life for the better? If you are the only one who understands it, you will not go far. Or if it is not your passion, you risk being seen as a phony.

After Mitch determined there was no way Indiana could ever pay for all the road projects on the books and our only state toll road was losing money, leasing the asset made the most sense (as in dollars and cents), but he knew it would take a lot of retail selling.

Inside the State House limestone walls, everyone in the governor's office thought leasing a failing toll road to operators who had experience efficiently operating roads all over the world would be well-received in the legislature. Not so fast, said the opposition. A lot of emotional, prejudicial rhetoric hit the fan.

We scheduled town hall meetings in every county through which the toll road runs and, true to form, Mitch became his own spokesman. Packed crowds turned out and expressed their displeasure; many people were finger- pointing mad. Throughout the storm, however, not one person said he wanted to increase taxes, borrow more money, or not build roads. So in effect, folks were saying, "We do not like your idea, but we do not have one of our own."

Surprisingly, fence-sitters left the town hall meetings better educated and the issue had been defused in their minds. They came to understand that the new operator would be held to terms of a contract the same as the companies that pour the concrete or supply the state with paper. In the end, after all the fear-mongering and demagoguing, it did not make one iota of difference in Mitch's reelection. In fact, four years later he increased his margin of victory, and an analysis by *Barron's* magazine talked about what a great deal Indiana got in leasing the road when we did.

The same type of travel was required when the Indianapolis Colts sought to build a new stadium and the capital city looked to build a much needed larger convention center. When the team ran out of ideas and the city could not get it across the goal line, they called the Governor and asked for help. After significant research, he pledged to take the cause to the streets and convince the surrounding region to help.

Again, town hall meetings were hosted in neighboring counties, the Governor met with all county commissioners, and the case was made that in order to compete and qualify for the biggest national conventions, we would need a bigger convention center. That would require their buy-in and investment. With the bigger conventions would come more hotel rooms and more people eating at their local restaurants. Only after town hall after town hall, the initiative passed and because of it, Lucas Oil Stadium hosted the 2012 Super Bowl, the granddaddy of them all.

Joe South's 1960s song, Walk a Mile in My Shoes, goes, "If you could see through my eyes instead of your ego...."

SEVEN

Be Inclusive

MITCH LONG ENJOYED THE support of formidable coalitions, both typical and atypical interest groups. Because of his reaching-out approach, he got the backing of union building trades as well as the state Chamber of Commerce, the Manufacturer's Association, and the National Federation of Independent Businesses. The Fraternal Order of Police and prominent veteran leaders were seen on campaign ads, pledging their support in their own nonpartisan words. In 2008, the International Association of Fire Fighters supported both Mitch, a Republican for Governor and Barack Obama, a Democrat for President.

The late Congresswoman Julia Carson, a longtime icon of Indianapolis, gave a "My Man Mitch" shout-out at the biggest Black Expo in the nation. While Mitch and Julia had their policy disagreements, their mutual respect for each other's commitments to improving lives was a model her son Sam Carson often talked about. In 2008, African American community activists distributed

Governor Daniels "suggestion boxes" to inner city barbershops and hair salons.

So it was not surprising that in 2008, Mitch received twenty percent of the African American vote, up thirteen percent from 2004. After four years of attending events, he was not just talking the talk during a campaign. To put this in perspective, in 2004, first-time candidate, Daniels lost Marion County, the state's largest county and capital city, by 18,000 and yet won it four years later by 48,000 votes. Daniels received 7,000 more votes in Center Township than he had in 2004, up ten percent. Center Township is the heart of Marion County and was newly represented by Julia's grandson, D-Rep. Andre Carson, in the US Congress. Daniels received 31.6 percent of the votes from African American majority precincts throughout Indianapolis and received 71,000 more votes in Marion County than the 2008 GOP Presidential candidate Senator John McCain.

While some advised Mitch not to spend time in certain areas of the state, such as East Chicago where eighty percent of the vote was Latino, Mitch instead went and shared his One Indiana message. Fluent in Spanish, he earned the support of traditionally Democrat leaning Latino voters who also were concerned about jobs, the economy, and education.

Like it or not, most citizens want their elected officials to work across party and ethnic lines. White suburbanites appreciated the fact that a candidate paid attention not only to their Starbucks-dotted corners but to the inner city as well. If you will not go there and share your well thought out message, who will plant the seeds that one day may sprout?

By making coalition-building a practice, goals that once seemed impossible ultimately can be reached. Lonely and lofty objectives gain traction through coalition cooperation. For example, Joe Kernan, the incumbent turned out by Mitch in

2004, agreed at Mitch's request to co-chair a bipartisan effort for local government reform, one of Mitch's most important legislative goals. Later the losing candidate in the 2008 Democratic primary joined Mitch in an effort to raise funds to rebuild an historic covered bridge that had been destroyed in a severe weather storm. Mitch had always worked hard to include those who shared a same goal, whether or not they shared different goals the rest of the time.

No leader will enjoy one hundred percent approval from the people, ever. Get past it. Work with those who agree with you and hold out hope that those who disagree will come around through education, or at least will give you an opportunity to prove them wrong. Stay on the high road, because if you take the low road and burn your bridges, odds are you will regret it later. Some things are better left unsaid when disagreement dominates a discussion and negotiations fail.

On the other hand, praising supporters not only recognizes their value, it also encourages others to join. The reward given for their input and resources will multiply in part because everyone wants to be part of the winning team and appreciates being recognized. There is strength in numbers, so start and always continue adding to and maintaining your list of helpers.

From day one, Mitch encouraged supporters to sign the exterior of RV1. This gave folks the feel of buy-in, of being part of something big. The campaign organized around sixty coalition groups of supporters from union members to teachers to small business owners to sportsmen. One loyal and longtime friend of Daniels jokingly said that the governor even had the support of all the left-handed, smallmouth bass fishermen in Indiana.

One of the most common mistakes many candidates make is to believe that once they have a group's support, it is forever. Not true.

Coalition maintenance requires constant attention and involvement. If you do not ask for support and take the time to explain why you would appreciate their help, someone else will. Believing you have paid your dues to one group or another is fantasy.

Another mistake is accepting your predecessor's experiences, of either party, and opinions as your own. Be the creator of your own alliances. If you are on opposite sides one year and won without them, consider forgiving them and offering an olive branch. As Mitch always said, *"I'm too lazy to carry a grudge."* It is disarming and gracious. Rarely is a second chance to join the winning team ignored.

A key and subtle byproduct of strong coalition support comes when you are attacked. When your competitors malign you, your defenders also feel attacked and they step forward. When your opponents say you are a bully and do not listen, their words will fall on deaf ears because so many are standing with you. Ultimately, empty rhetoric is just that.

Do not just think outside of the box, expand the box. Use your candidacy to help coalition groups get fired up, and recruit new members by working on your shared issues.

In 2008, Mitch won southern Indiana big, by fifty-seven percent. Southern Indiana was known as Blue Dog, once called Reagan Democrat territory, and was for a long time represented in Congress by Democrats, such as Representatives Lee Hamilton, Frank McCloskey, Baron Hill and Brad Ellsworth. In 2008, Hill also won reelection fifty-seven to thirty-eight percent and Ellsworth was reelected sixty-four to thirty-five percent.

In addition, Mitch won every county in the blue-collar UAW region (Howard, Grant, Madison, Delaware), an improvement from 2004.

We could not keep the famous green "My Man Mitch" tee shirts in stock on college campuses. Mitch was able to articulate a substantive message to the generation who will inherit our debt or savings in a way that was cool and fun. It is not every day that your candidate for governor strikes up the band or rides in on his Harley in jeans and a tee shirt and is able to discuss any issue mentioned that day in *The Wall Street Journal*.

Mitch made it a habit to stay connected to various communities by going where the locals themselves went. Before attending Indianapolis' annual Black Expo and the Circle City parade, Mitch started the day at the Country Kitchen, a famous diner in an Indianapolis African American community. High-fives and "My Man Mitch" chants were part of the proceedings.

Because he was the first governor to start recognizing and hosting the Iftar Muslim annual event at the State House and one year at the Governor's Residence, the Indiana Muslim Association presented Mitch with their Distinguished Hoosier Muslim award. Iftar is the evening meal after sundown when Muslims gather to break their fast during Ramadan.

Mitch also attended the American Institute Awards Gala, where he was introduced by President Obama's US Secretary of Transportation and longtime Mitch friend, Ray LaHood, to keynote their gathering in Washington, DC.

Being governor and responsible to over six million people means you must be able to speak to those you may or may not agree with on every issue.

When asked to speak at the nonpartisan Indiana Leadership Prayer Breakfast, Mitch delivered the following extemporaneous remarks in February 2008.

"Those of us in this room who are temporarily tasked with public responsibility serve people of faith and those of no belief equally. We respect them equally. We must love them, whatever their view of us.

"There are very many people, many good people, good Samaritans that reject the idea of any power larger than themselves. They would tell you that they serve their neighbor and do good deeds out of reason; it is simply wiser to organize society when people treat each other with care. Or, that there are evolutionary instincts which lead us to cooperation: this is better for the success of the species long term. But there are far more powerful, and far more prevalent biological urges that lead humans—fallen humans—to cruelty and to selfishness and disregard of the neighbor in need on the road.

"The man on the road to Jericho was not responding to a biological urge. He didn't reason his way to the good deed that he did. He didn't say I will help this man and one day he will help me in return. He didn't say I will help this man or else maybe he will one day decide to harm me. The Good Samaritan answered to a voice in the heart—a voice placed there by a Creator who loves us and instructs us to love each other. Not because it is in our self interest, not because we have reasoned our way to this conclusion, but because it is right and it is just and it is as He wills it."

The Major Moves initiative was the benficiary of Mitch's coalition building. There is no question that without the broad-based support of unusual bed-fellows, such as the teamsters, sheet-metal workers, carpenters, operating engineers, as well as realtors, chambers, concrete and pavement guys, economic development corporations, growth councils, county commissioners, banks, mayors Republican and Democrat, bricklayers, electricians, IN Motor Truck Association and Indiana Manufacturers, the Major Moves program never would have happened.

Former Democrat Mayor of Terre Haute, Kevin Burke, expressed his support at a Major Moves press conference in the governor's office by saying, "I've never seen a bag of Democrat or Republican cement." He was speaking about jobs and community projects he had worked on for years, not politics.

Because not a single Democrat Indiana State Representative or State Senator supported leasing the toll road, Republican legislators got cover from the union trades who traditionally only supported Democrats. One of the last of the building trades to sign on Major Moves was the Indiana Laborers and their late nationally-known leader, Jerry Lee.

During the 2004 campaign, Jerry Lee taught me his three F's of campaigning. He told me in his Terre Haute local union hall office, "Eric, you can "f__k" (rhymes with duck), fight or flight; it's your choice." Meaning we could be friends, we could duke it out or I could run away. Now, fast-forward to after the election. Jerry Lee invited me for a second time, along with the newly elected Lieutenant Governor Becky Skillman, to meet with his leadership in their union hall basement. Although it was midday, the smoke was thick, the beer plentiful, and he could not have made us more welcome.

This labor leader and the Governor could hardly have stood farther apart when we started, but through working together on the biggest road program in our state's history, we found common ground and mutual respect as well as job prospects for Jerry Lee's union members.

Months later, I was invited to attend this legendary man's funeral as the Governor's representative. I was possibly the sole Republican in the funeral home.

In case running for governor didn't work out, Mitch had a fall back plan.

*Hoosier hospitality includes giving directions to Mitch, the perpetual
state traveler, as he searches for the area's best tenderloin.*

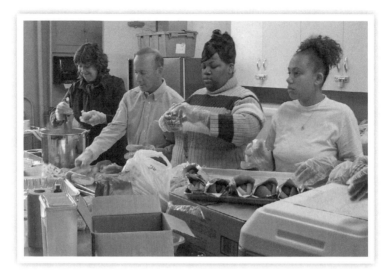

No matter how big or small the task, always assemble the best team for the job.

Even man's best friend sported the brand (Mutts for Mitch).

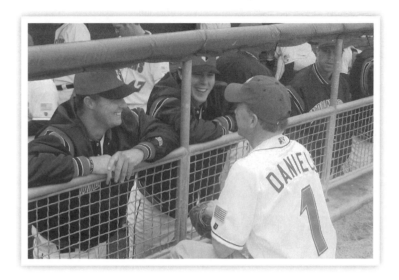

Always be suited up and ready to go.

Telling tall tales with new friends.

Careful betting against the guy off the street.

Think big and outside your borders.

Without the courage to see your vision through,
you might not ever realize favorable results.

EIGHT

Be Bold and Willing to Aggravate

IF YOU HAVE NEVER second-guessed yourself or asked, "Did we do too much," then you probably were not aiming high enough. If you do not have bumper stickers and websites against you, then you are probably not pushing it. If the naysayers are not trying to discourage and defeat you, you are not rocking the boat. The bigger you are, the tougher your competition will be on you and it will know no boundaries.

It is as true in corporate America as it is in politics. When a company becomes uber successful, it becomes a target of those losing market share. Think about Nike, Walmart, and Starbucks over the years. You are probably playing it too safe if you are not thinking about equation changers. It is necessary and possible to take risks without being reckless. Most successful leaders fail along the way. If you want to move the needle, think big and act on your ideas.

Sure, going for the long ball will draw predictable criticisms. You will hear you are a bulldozer, you do not listen, and you are irresponsible. But if you are willing to be controversial and even temporarily unpopular, you are saying to defenders of the status quo, "Not on my watch." You are saying to those who have a defeatist attitude, "No more." Reform by its very nature means there will be change and significant change will upset the complacent.

When Mitch was elected, he laid out an audacious first-year agenda and followed up with a second-year jaw-dropping agenda. To everyone's surprise in year three, after watching the State House fall into opposition Party hands, everyone thought Mitch would opt for a lay-up agenda. Instead, he innovated and initiated, collaborating to pass legislation in healthcare and education and promoting more private-public partnerships to build roads.

To truly jump out front, innovating and initiating go hand in hand. Do both. Again, be willing to fail. In fact, Mitch once told me he was perfectly prepared to be "one and done."

Do you think the Wright brothers and Thomas Edison were not willing to fail? Agencies should be expected to try new things. In the Daniels Administration, agencies were free to be innovative and by doing so, saved over $200 million. In short, go big early, or go home.

> "He's been bold, controversial, almost fearless. He's been willing to advance his agenda even though he has suffered a great deal of criticism along the way...." (Robert Schmuhl, University of Notre Dame, professor of American Studies)

> "It seems likely that he is a governor of consequence, a governor who has made things happen...." (James Madison, Indiana University historian and author)

Just after getting elected, Mitch's equal employment opportunity policy angered right-wing voters when he said the state executive branch would not discriminate against an employee's sexual orientation, gender identity, race, color, religion, sex, national origin, ancestry, age, disability or veteran status. I can remember vividly all those constituent emails, letters and conservative e-newsletters that took exception with a policy that stood against discrimination; however, Mitch never flinched. The policy had never been about granting special rights, and it did not cause any problems afterward in hiring or firing as many predicted.

Another "much ado about nothing" issue came about when the governor announced that although he and the First Lady would raise the necessary private funds and donated labor to completely refurbish the official Governor's Residence, they did not want to live full-time just down the street from their own family home. They would keep the Residence open for the public for Garden Club meetings, receptions and other special events. In addition, the First Lady would keep her offices in the official Residence.

In the end, although a vocal minority thought the Governor should respectfully observe tradition and move into the Residence, the public at large appreciated the fact that someone was willing to take on the job of renovating and modernizing the house at no taxpayer expense so others could enjoy the facility and not worry about the leaking roof, wiring hazards, and the inefficient heating and cooling. Private contributors and contract labor donated over $1 million for an extreme makeover. The Residence belonged to the people, and pride in the facility was restored. Most thought the Governor was old enough to determine where he would live and sleep.

The Governor stayed at the Residence when work called for it. For instance, on the rare occasions when a violent offender faced execution in Indiana, the governor remained overnight at the Residence so he could quickly respond to any court orders.

Another prickly issue steeped in tradition arose as soon as the governor announced his recommendation to close the Indiana Soldiers' and Sailors' Children's Home and change its mission. Although the governor had good relations with various veterans groups, no amount of reasoning would appease the state's proud and accomplished American Legion. For whatever reason, including tradition, Indiana was the last state in the nation not to make the tough call away from housing troubled youth far from their home community, until Mitch. Protests, rallies, a Facebook page and letter-writing campaign were initiated against the Governor's Office. A senior-level person at the American Legion even took it upon himself to make this his personal cause. However, no one bought their arguments and a move was made to transform the property.

Shortly thereafter, the Indiana National Guard moved onto the property in 2010, and brought its full-scale program for at-risk Hoosier teenagers to the site. The program began to serve more youth at a lower cost and kept the military commitment to the community.

Some people wear it on their sleeve; Mitch puts it on his bike.

Young Hoosiers had a vested interest and predominant role in Mitch's campaign from day one, like this rally in Whitley County, Indiana.

NINE

Focus Relentlessly on Results; Measure Everything

ONCE ELECTED, IT IS tempting to go-along to get-along. Doing the right thing is usually the hardest path and may cause you to lose friends. Have the facts ready so the next time your allies threaten to withdraw their support, you can provide them with evidence that you are on the right track. Protectors of the status quo do not take a day off; neither can champions of reform.

In fact, the reformer's work is never done. As good as you get, you must keep aiming higher every year or complacency will set in. Each new day brings new knowledge, new markets and new competitors impatient to take the lead. Think about these inspirational Indiana entrepreneurs: Madame C. J. Walker, legendary and successful manufacturer of hair care and cosmetics for African American women; Michael Graves, world-renowned architect and product designer; and Eli Lilly, founder of the giant pharmaceutical company.

The obvious common denominator among them all was their insatiable desire to innovate and to be the best at serving their customers. To accomplish that, companies have to communicate with their teams and persist in measuring the value and services they provide.

Mitch always said: "If you are not keeping score, you're just practicing" and "What gets measured gets done."

In the quest for the number one spot, you will be up against constant resistance and at times, you will fail. Mitch took chance after chance after chance. After every victory, he went for the next one, never playing it safe when many candidates would have been satisfied with an above sixty percent approval rating. He was after better government for less, but if something that was urgently needed cost more, he did it, such as hiring hundreds of child protection caseworkers to save at-risk children.

"State government is leaner and cleaner, and more taxpayer-friendly. The size of state government has been reduced by more than 10 percent, over 4,000 employees. Even though we have raised worker pay more than in previous years, it costs taxpayers less to meet the payroll of state government today than it did in 2004." (Again, these numbers went further up later, topping 5,000 as the months unfolded after this *State of the State Address*.)

"And government's service to taxpayers is provably, measurably better. A new crew of people from outside government has been at work in departments large and small on a mission to make government work for people. Twenty thousand more single parents now receive the child support they're owed. Public retirees now receive their first pension check without delay. Taxpayers' refund checks come back in half the time. Two hundred seventy-five more state policemen are on the roads and fighting crime. There are hundreds of such examples. But let's examine just one that captures and typifies them all.

"Last month, the average total visit time at an Indiana BMV license branch was – anyone care to guess? – eight minutes, 11 seconds. Statewide, the customer satisfaction rating was 96 percent. And that's among those who had to go to a branch at all.

"You can now do almost all your business by mail, or Internet, and get a discount for doing so. You can register a new vehicle at the dealer, rather than making a second trip to a branch. If you have to go in person, you can check online and see exactly how long the visit times are right now at every branch near you. Or, you can make an appointment, so when you get there, you don't wait at all.

"These improvements did not come quickly, or easily. We made mistakes along the way; some experiments worked poorly, and were abandoned. Some changes, like most changes in life, aroused concern and discontent. But the results are real, and dramatic. I dwell on this one example because, as most Hoosiers readily understand, if our people can fix the BMV, they can fix anything.

"Because of a stronger economy, and businesslike stewardship of government, our fiscal situation is also profoundly better. The bankruptcy of three years ago is far behind us." (Governor Mitch Daniels, *2008 State of the State Address*)

At the same time that Indiana added more child protection caseworkers and state policemen and passed a long-overdue additional veteran benefits bill, the state also reported a healthy rainy day reserve balance rather than the budget shortfalls shared by surrounding states. Despite strong resistance to aggressive proposals at the time, the results confirmed again and again that Indiana was better off than all its surrounding states.

Daniels proved that results do matter and do trump the obstructionists. He talked about real accomplishments and these same accomplishments earned him and Indiana various national awards, including *Governing Magazine*'s Public Official of the Year award and the Sunny Award for superior efforts to bring transparency to government through better accessibility of state websites.

The Sunny Award was given to only 214 government entities out of over 6,000 government websites analyzed for proactive disclosure of information regarding budgets, meetings, lobbying, financial audits, contracts, academic performance, public records, and taxes.

In 2012, for the second year in a row, Indiana received an A-from both *The Sunshine Review,* a national nonpartisan government transparency agency, and US PIRG, a transparency site that rated Indiana's transparency portal third best in the country.

"Making state government more transparent has been one of our priorities for more than seven years. We'll continue our push to be a national leader in operating an open and honest government," Mitch said.

But it is not just the squeaky wheels that need attention. Many times it is small unattended issues that evolve and explode. You must manage them early before they become big problems. To do that, it is helpful to set up a tracking system of all departments or agencies. Labeling with green (good), yellow (caution) and red (needs immediate help) will identify, predict, and forecast trouble areas by past performance. It also gives you ample time to get new eyes on old problems and circle the wagons to address a troubled asset.

Once the trouble area is identified, gather your most innovative and experienced teammates and play through how you will improve. In the yellow zone, it may be as simple as replacing someone on the line or on the top floor who is not performing. Red zone corrections call for more drastic approaches and typically a more radical remedy.

Be frugal in all matters, even when righting the ship. Micromanaging the budget sets an example for everyone to see. Your team should know that you sweat the small stuff, so they need to fix it before it gets to you. If you are measuring the cost of coffee, paper, and pens, folks are less likely to splurge on golden faucets. If they do, make an example of the splurge.

For Mitch, frugality came naturally. When he took up golf, he wore a garden glove instead of investing in a golf glove. There's a guy you want to select in a pick-up game of golf. A garden glove is so outrageous, he must be a hustler, so pick him!

Speaking of measuring, it is critical you also measure your timelines and always know precisely when the first, second, third and fourth quarters of your legislative session begin and end. Getting a $3.85 billion lease deal done in 117 days was not easy but would have been next to impossible if we had not managed the time we had.

Measuring outcomes of government activity tells the electorate you are taking responsibility, especially when you share the results, good and bad. This transparency will earn the taxpayers' trust and boost your credibility.

When Mitch began to study the Gary Airport, we learned some flights had only eleven passengers a day. Northwest Indiana on the outskirts of Chicago, had the potential to be one of Indiana's regional engines, but it needed to change its business model to fully maximize its advantages, which included its location and people power.

Everyone working for the administration or organization needs to know his work will be viewed by the press, the public, even partisan opponents in Quarterly Progress Reports.

This reporting system creates a way to measure everyone's progress or lack thereof so there are no surprises if a change needs to be made. When Mitch first took over, he created a tiger team, a small group of five budget hawks who constantly evaluated what every agency was doing. These budget hawks did not report to the agency, just to the Governor and Budget Director. Turf-builders resent having someone come into their shop and recommend changes, but the creative heads welcome different perspectives and encourage new ways to address old problems.

Working together, even relying on "the bad guy from the budget office is making us do this," helped our Department of Natural Resources (DNR) to eliminate one hundred percent of its permit backlog. Afterward, seventy-one percent of its properties made money, up from sixty-seven percent when Mitch assumed office, and the state inns were full because business models had changed to adapt. Taxpayers will pay for state accommodations if they are clean and safe. The Indiana Department of Environmental Management caught up on its permit backlog as well.

The total revenue brought in by Indiana State Parks and Reservoirs, grew from just over $18 million in 2004 to $25 million in 2010.

And Indiana became a state of trails and recreational opportunities, publishing its first greenways plan, "*Hoosiers on the Move,*" in 2006. The plan outlined 180 miles of rail converted to trails across Indiana, uniting every Hoosier within fifteen minutes of a trail. The full and completed plan has over 2,000 miles of interconnected trails and bikeways.

For years outdoorsmen, politicians, and landowners had tried to figure out a way to purchase farmland known as Goose Pond in southwestern Indiana. Bird watchers, trappers, and hunters viewed the terrain as one of the few areas in the country that had the capability to change migratory patterns if kept intact and not sold off piecemeal. In the fall of 2005, when the Indiana Department of Natural Resources announced the land deal, with the assistance of various other organizations, the DNR had acquired over 8,000 acres, creating the Goose Pond Fish and Wildlife Area. As they say at the DNR, "We're in the business of making memories," and to visit the Goose Pond area is to never forget it.

Not satisfied, during the summer of 2010, Mitch announced a massive 43,000-acre conservation project along 94 miles of the Wabash River and Sugar Creek. He followed up with a second project targeting more than 70,000 acres along the Muscatatuck River, known as Muscatatuck Bottoms, sprawling across three counties and Sugar Creek.

Mitch said, "We're out to create something of lasting and large importance for our state and protect its natural beauty. With these projects, we aim to make Indiana a destination point for waterfowl, a destination point for tourists, and to become a national leader in wetlands and wildlife protection."

In March, 2011, Mitch received the Wetland Conservation Award from Ducks Unlimited.

But he did not stop. In December of 2011, he announced another 1,250 acres, formerly state prison property, would become the largest public wild bird habitat to be funded by revenue generated by contract farmers on 100 acres of the property.

Indiana set these records for protecting natural resources and beauty at the same time the federal Environmental Protection Agency recognized Indiana had improved its air quality and still fixed the permitting process at I.D.E.M.

These kids will never know how long it took to get their piece of the interstate. After discussions since the 1950s about building the southwestern leg of I-69, ground was finally broken at Evansville on July 17, 2008, for the 142-mile project.

TEN

Do Not Take the Bait; Stay Disciplined and Positive

REMAIN POSITIVE, REFUSE TO go negative and always remember that ideas and commitment matter and will trump a superficial, nasty campaign if you stay committed to the plan. The opposition will be tempted to paint you in a negative light, but in the long run, this strategy usually proves terminal for them if you stay above it.

From day one, Mitch insisted on running only principled and positive campaigns. Both his general election opponents ran all-negative-all-the-time campaigns and the contrast was stark. Not only was this a positive versus negative match, it was also a contrast of the future versus the past.

Mitch's overwhelming reelection proved that the vision of his ideas, the courage in which he pursued them, and the results that flowed from their fruition mattered most. It is hard to argue with the method that gave Mitch more votes than anyone who has ever run for office in Indiana.

It takes discipline when you have to react to a gotcha scenario or negative attack. Answer hard and loud, then move on and stick to your campaign plan. It is your character being tested, your integrity. Do not sink to their level; contrast it. Contrasting is okay. Defending the high ground is endless, no matter what day, week, month, or year it is. In today's world, blogs, YouTube, and Twitter take the place of communication between real people.

In 2008, many people thought our opponent's mouth piece was the most malicious woman in Indiana politics. Nothing seemed off limits in their quest to throw mud and see if anything would stick. But in the end, voters wondered why the opposition had focused on these tactics instead of offering what its team would do if given the opportunity to govern.

Doing what is right counts with the independent-minded public. If I had a nickel for every time I heard, "You guys could afford to stay positive, we can't," I could retire. If you are trying to get away with something, you are walking on a tightrope with no net, and one day, it will catch up to you. The embarrassment or cover-up is always worse than the original crime in politics. As always, honesty is the best policy and over time, it always prevails.

When Mitch first decided to work for President Bush, he immediately sold all his stock and put remaining investments into a blind trust to prevent conflicts of interest. This rule is in place to prevent insider trading and protect against accusations of impropriety. As a candidate, Mitch came under intense criticism for once owning IPALCO Stock and selling it before the company lost a significant amount of its value.

Opponents tried to make the case that as a company board member, Mitch should have lost money and not sold his stock, even though he had to sell as a requirement for accepting the appointment as the President's budget director. The opposition ran hard-hitting television commercials, attacking Mitch's character in attempts to discredit him.

Mitch's opponents never let up, as if they did not realize the effects of negative action on the party. Their purpose revolved around obstruction and tearing down, not building up of anything.

Again, the best way to stay positive is to have a plan and stick to it. A common mistake leaders unconsciously make is trying to appear as if they are omniscient by pretending to own every problem a reporter or opponent brings up. Leaders complicate their positions by commenting on issues not in their area of influence and for which they do not have all the facts at the time of the interview.

If it is not part of your core mission, refer the reporters to an expert. If you do not have all the facts and you need them, say so and then get back to them. Do not dismiss or deny something that might be true and certainly do not embellish the truth either. If you are second, do not say you are first. Reporters make it their business to prove you wrong and once they expose a vulnerability or a mistake, they always watch for the next slip-up.

Overplaying your hand also invites skepticism and more significantly lessens your credibility. When it comes time to list your victories and accomplishments for those invested in your enterprise, you want people to trust what you say. Claiming exaggerated results may work at the press conference, but upon further review and digested thoroughly, any advance is erased at the next press conference, and there will be a next press conference.

After the 2010 elections, Indiana Republicans went from forty-eight members out of one hundred in the Indiana House of Representatives to sixty. The new and emboldened majority went from minority to strong majority overnight. The new majority came to town in early January 2011, with the purpose of shaking up the status quo, including education reform.

The various reform ideas that had been bottled up for decades became a possibility. The opponents of such reforms reinforced their reputations as champions of the status quo versus the promoter of ideas and different results.

The public understandably responded by supporting progressive-minded legislators who were willing to try something different in pursuit of improvement. Underscoring the need for reform brought together leaders from both parties, including Governor Mitch Daniels, President Barack Obama, and his Secretary of Education, Arnie Duncan. Duncan visited Indiana to support the state's commitment to education reform initiatives.

But that did not stop the entrenched professional special interest groups from organizing a massive misinformation effort. Teachers were led to believe they would be receiving a $900 pay cut if the education reforms passed. Email campaigns began hammering legislators who supported the reforms. Legislative town hall meetings were taken over by the education union network where protesters claimed those in favor of the reforms were against kids.

When the opposition claims you are against the elderly or children, that is a clue they are trying to bait you. You need to be able to articulate how the reforms you are pushing will improve the scores of students, not just settle old scores. Be able to describe how your initiatives will enable poor children to choose to attend a great school, just like the more affluent children already do. In 2012, after the decision was made to add Right to Work to the agendas of the Speaker of The House, the Senate Leader, and the Governor, the battle lines were drawn. One key component to becoming the first state in years to pass Right To Work legislation would be to have cooler heads prevailing when the sparks started to fly. I recall reminding folks "not to take their bait" and end up in the gutter. Right to Work is the Holy Grail of labor law and the arch rival of unions.

As predicted, union members were bussed in from out of state and paid to sit in the state house to protest a labor bill that gave workers the right to pay or not to pay union dues. This freedom was interpreted as a threat to union organizing.

Professional union hecklers jammed the State House during the governor's *State of the State Address* and tried to drown out his speech. When the governor attended an event to honor Martin Luther King, Jr., union members booed him and when the non-union building contractors attended state house hearings, union members surrounded them. They chanted "whore, whore, whore" at a female pro-Right To Work advocate and wrote with chalk on streets and sidewalks phrases, such as "KILL MITCH." But less than nine percent of Indiana's private sector work force was unionized and the other ninety-one percent rejected their antics. Republican legislators were galvanized by their behavior.

In the face of the hostility and threats to even shut down the Super Bowl, the pro-Right To Work coalition never lost its cool and remained professional. Follow the plan and stay disciplined. Also, remember those *against* something unfortunately are always louder than those *for* something.

No union member's pay or benefits were reduced and the infant mortality rate did not increase as Democrat legislators had outrageously claimed it would. The only thing that changed is that workers now have the choice of whether or not to pay union dues. As a result, companies that had not considered locating in Indiana because we were not a Right to Work state started to investigate the option of investing and bringing jobs to Indiana.

Find Mitch.

ELEVEN

Let Yourself Go and
Take Calculated Risks

LEADERS NEED TO TAKE calculated risks, both personally and professionally, in order to increase awareness and sharpen the ability to talk about anything with anyone. Total immersion in your constituency will reveal perspectives on issues you might never have contemplated. You will learn about the constituents themselves, what they care about, what they need most, and how they think.

Muster the courage and put yourself into impromptu settings, unfamiliar situations, and diverse environments as opposed to controlled environments. Again, Mitch stayed in homes rather than hotels so he would have down time with individuals and, incidentally, where he might get some real nitty gritty experiences far away from the special interest groups. Traveling in RV1 promoted the power of these impromptu stops along the way.

Do not become dependent on binders with schedules,

backgrounds of every person and place, and speeches to read. You need to learn to improvise when you are challenged and just as importantly, when you are praised. You can also learn how to respond with equanimity to adversity and setbacks that are bound to come up when you do not play it safe all the time. You can learn to recover quickly.

Stepping out of your comfort zone prepares you to deal with unexpected situations, people who agree with you and people who do not, people who do not even make sense, or who do not understand the facts. It allows you to learn at your own pace, rather than when a fight is brought to you and you are taken by surprise. Professionally, Mitch always included events where no governor of his party had ever attended.

Yes, there will be mistakes made when you put yourself out there, but you will learn from them much more than if you had been playing it safe. And mistakes bring you and your team closer as a family when you learn together.

Do not try to do it all. Leaders need to delegate and groom future leaders, a duty that is many times the most important legacy. Even if you are your best press secretary, political director, campaign manager, and/or speech writer, do not stunt the organizational growth of your team. Doing everyone else's job keeps you from maximizing your own. If you are taking on subsidiary roles and not accepting counsel, hire new help. Talented people will be drawn to you, but only if you respect and encourage their talent. Micromanaging department heads tends to attract staff that requires micromanage-ment!

Grow thick skin. The bigger you are, the bigger the target you make for your detractors. The more aggressive your timeline, the more controversial your goals will appear, and therefore, the more you will be attacked. There have been many politicians who soared temporarily with high approval ratings by doing nothing because they wanted to be liked more than they wanted to get something done. Do not overreact to the vocal minority, but do respond, and never appear rattled. Instead of lashing back, confidently respond with the facts. Learn to ignore slanderous attacks and insults. If you appear to have a glass jaw, your opponents will constantly throw punches, hoping one lands and it may only take one to turn the tide. Find a way to deal with the criticism and then move to the next item.

Stop reading letters to the editor and unqualified bloggers' opinions of you. Your mood should not be altered by professional blowhards. Nowadays with the internet, anyone who has a thought can type. We all knew Mitch read a dozen sources everyday, usually before breakfast. If someone forwarded him a nasty letter to the editor or a photo of a rude bumper sticker, such as "Ditch Mitch" and "F#$k Mitch," he asked, "So what are you going to do about it?"

Adjectives that were used to describe the governor included: small, stiff, short, pale, unimposing, unassuming, uninspiring, understated, uncharismatic, accountant-like, non-telegenic, boring, balding, blunt, nerdy, wooden, wonky, puny and pint-sized. The man portrayed was wise to keep his sense of humor.

Smiling, I was fond of asking the detractors, "How does it feel to be part of such a small minority, completely out of touch with how the majority feels?" That usually defused the incident and circumvented time lost, dealing with petty concerns.

The last thing you want to do is snap or melt down under pressure. Your staff will take on your personality because your team is an extension of you. You cannot afford to foment a crisis. Mitch did not suffer fools lightly and expected staff to hold the line when fools came into view.

Always keep your sense of humor. It can serve you in many situations, like the time Mitch told a Washington crowd, "Our morbidly obese federal government needs not just behavior modification but bariatric surgery. You'd be amazed how much government you'll never miss."

And Mitch was a man who could also deliver it. "I bring greetings from my beloved Indiana," he said once. "South Bend is in the north, North Vernon's in the south, and French Lick is not what you hoped it was."

Do not forget to have fun. If you are not comfortable enough to enjoy events and have fun, you will look like a big phony in the photographs everyone is taking of you. It is easy to look like you are having a blast when you really are. Let go, and let people get to know you as you really are.

Genuinely have fun, and you'll look comfortable doing so. Every Halloween the Governor, the First Lady and former and current staff members dressed up at the Governor's Residence and handed out treats. One year Mitch was a cast member from *Grease* and another year, the Cowardly Lion from the *The Wizard of Oz*.

Always looking for different themed events, Mitch rode in a fast-track go-cart or his Harley with eight hundred of his riding buddies behind him. Tailgating before a college football game was a must-do, and he was always ready to throw out the first pitch, take the microphone during half time, or call high school basketball when asked.

In June 2004, *Indy Men's Magazine* said it best. "Mitch Daniels: devoted family man, wildly charismatic, funny as hell and bright as all get-out. Daniels' campaign, like its campaigner, is refreshingly devoid of pretense and mean-spiritedness."

When you visit college campuses, do a Q&A with the students without pre-screened questions. Encourage students to ask anything. Occasionally you will get a student who asks an embarrassing question, but if you are comfortable and not paranoid, the ease with which you honestly answer will surprise the whole audience.

When you write op eds, do your own writing. If you prepare your own speeches, they sound more like you. I would encourage you, however, to have your staff comment, anticipate questions and provide background research.

There will be many opportunities for you to participate in events even outside your comfort zone. Mitch was invited to attend the National Gridiron, where the President headlines, throwing jabs at reporters and the other two guest speakers. When Mitch accepted, he knew Saturday Night Live-quality humor would be required and that the President would have the best sketch artists helping him write his routine. The governor, in an arm sling after rotator cuff surgery, told President Obama, "Until this thing comes off, I can cling to my gun, or my Bible, but not both." Mitch was referring to a well-known gaff candidate Obama made in Pennsylvania on the campaign trail.

These events have little upside but can have a huge downside because we tend to remember best the folks who bombed. Another bombing opportunity was presented to Mitch in 2012, when he was asked to deliver the Republican response to President Obama's *State of the Union* address.

Mitch stood in front of an American flag, without a podium, a risky plan perhaps but not unlike most of Mitch's plans. He flawlessly delivered his twelve-minute response to Obama's one-hour and five-minute speech.

On the first day of the first campaign, Mitch charged our

little band of brothers and sisters who had assembled on RV1 to simply "make friends along the way." Our goal was always understood as multiply our troops, not divide and conquer.

It is imperative that the team keeps a positive attitude and has fun along the way, even though it is hard to turn around a bankrupt state and tough to persuade those who have spent a lifetime voting against your team. Nothing can replace an *esprit de corps*. That reminds me, I used to have a Navy commander who jokingly said, "All liberty is secured until morale improves."

Hard work never seems to get old when value is placed on creativity, with input from every person, and the team is enthusiastic about the cause. Young volunteers thrive in a fun place in which to work and grow. Stifling them will lead to an old staff and a perspective biased toward the way things used to be done. You never know what you will learn from your next trip or meeting with our country's next generation. Since they are going to be stuck with the national debt, it is only fair they get a seat at the table.

Some campaigns and businesses rely on young folks because experience costs more, but even if you can afford veterans, it is smart to over-compensate with younger perspectives. Mitch used various ways to stay in touch with the twenty-to-thirty-somethings through events scheduled on college campuses or those geared toward young professionals. If you have a debate, invite a hundred young folks and watch the energy light up in your favor. Methodically visit every college campus in your state and ask the students questions. Attend high school athletic games, both boys' and girls'. Get your message out via Facebook and Twitter. Relying on network television spots, radio and direct mail is a failing formula for connecting with this key demographic group.

There will be numerous opportunities for staff to come

together and not talk shop, but if you do not schedule staff events, they will not happen. Campaigns are hectic, often chaotic, and staff will be pulled from one crisis to the next. The work by definition is never done until the polls close on election day.

So, assign someone the informal duty to act as the social chair, responsible for planning a few events, at a minimum, that will occur throughout the duration of the campaign. Start with an overnight retreat at a state park inn, where the policy shop can get to know the fundraisers, without their laptops staring at them. Always break for an hour to recognize holidays and going-away receptions for key staff. At the Governor's General Counsel's going-away party, I walked into the Governor's office in my red Union Jack pajamas, a reenactment of the counsel's nocturnal habit of sleeping at the office.

We later organized a hilarious "Dumb and Dumber" skit, making fun of the Governor's two advance guys and all the near-fatal staffing decisions they had made. Baseball games and race tracks are perfect venues for team-building. I am not a big race fan but it is hard not to have fun with twenty coworkers at the Anderson Night of Thrills, watching school bus demolition derby/crazy eight races. These gatherings present chances to remember and roast your friends and many times make the best friend photos.

Each gathering is the time to remind staff that they are part of what makes the team special and different. Because of their individual contribution, the team becomes stronger and everyone should derive a sense of pride from his or her team status.

Never settle for anything less than a bull's eye.

TWELVE

Always Aim Higher,
As Difficult As It May Be

ON ELECTION NIGHT, 2008, Mitch only had to wait two minutes (7:02 p.m. when all the polls had closed) to learn he had won, receiving more votes than anyone who had ever run for office in Indiana history. He was at the official Governor's Residence, just a few miles north of where he would later be celebrating with supporters. I interrupted the small dinner with his wife and a couple of lifelong friends.

"Governor, the race has been called," I said. "Congratulations!"

He excused himself from the table and stepped into the adjacent room with me. "By how much?" he asked.

"Fifty-three percent right now," I replied.

"Not good enough," he said, almost if it were some banana republic election and increasing his lead was as simple as finding another box stuffed with Daniels votes.

I said, "It's early and your lead will increase."

Which it did, all the way up to an eighteen-point victory. I later saw Cam Savage, the campaign communications director, at the victory celebration. We had talked about having the governor show up in time to be on the news live at twenty after or twenty before the hour in the nine or ten o'clock timeframe. We had no idea CNN and local media outlets would call the race so soon after the polls closed.

The it-must-be-better mentality is infectious – always wanting to do more, always wanting to improve. If you set out to break records, even your own, you just might. If you do not, you will not. So, we always looked to be the first and the best in the universe. Be the first to achieve and to reach beyond the potential. In doing so, you will lift up the state, past where it had fallen before.

Again, do not rest when you win. If you do, the staff will experience a letdown. Be team-oriented. Momentum feeds off itself. Always provide positive feedback during heated battles rather than taking a negative view of the outcome. Reinforcing words raise confidence.

Mitch once said, "We don't have a day to waste, let alone a session of the General Assembly, without making progress on big issues that might make this a greater state."

After a long drought with no positive feedback, call an all-staff meeting and praise the team's progress to put the wind back in everyone's sails, especially during those tense legislative stretches when all the chips are in and the stakes are high. Just like in business, especially in a tough market, let your employees know you have confidence in their work ethic and integrity, and that you know they will continue to challenge themselves with the goal of raising themselves and the company higher.

Never be satisfied.

From a national recession and tight budgets that resulted from the tough times, to major floods and tornadoes, the public considers how officials handle crises in deciding who will earn their votes. As much as the disasters themselves, the official responses to Exxon Valdez and Katrina were forever etched into the American memory. As I have said before, we learn from mistakes what works and what does not work. Unfortunate as they were, these crises taught anyone who was paying attention that the nation cannot afford to fumble and make mistakes of this magnitude ever again.

It was clear that Mitch was paying attention when floods and tornadoes hit Indiana, because he hit the ground running. Hoosiers gave Mitch high marks for his crisis management. After the horrific tornadoes that hit southern Indiana in March of 2012, he said the state's reaction was the fastest we had ever had. He also said in an interview with Bob Schieffer on "Face the Nation" that the weather service had given plenty of warning and that visiting the area, he had not talked to anyone who was not aware that the storms were on their way. The storm that devastated Henryville traveled at 175 miles per hour and stayed on the ground for fifty miles. When asked for an estimate of the amount of damage, Mitch said the sense of loss could not be measured in dollars. He said Hoosiers are tough and he had witnessed their resilience and can-do spirit. We should never be satisfied with the last lesson learned; there's always a next.

During Mitch's first term, he had gone to leaders of both large and small veteran groups, such as the American Legion, The Purple Heart Association, Veterans of Foreign Wars, and Disabled American Veterans to explain at the outset that he was serious about addressing the long-overdue benefits to Hoosier veterans.

He made it clear he was not going to just promise veterans agenda items he could not deliver. He planned to deliver. Mitch asked each group to compile its wish list, identify where there was overlap and show the fiscal impact on the budget that had for one reason or another in years past never been addressed.

The list Mitch ended up with and passed into law exempted from state income tax all military pay earned while serving in a combat theater; increased the maximum allowable state income tax deductions on military pay; provided state matching funds of up to $450,000 annually for Indiana Military Families Relief Fund, which was covered by a new "Support Our Troops" license plate; extended the delayed high school diploma program; allowed in-state tuition rates for out-of-state soldiers assigned to Indiana; created a Veterans Trust Fund; authorized the state's first full-time Women Veterans Coordinator; further enhanced transition practices and prioritized job placement for service men and women; increased the state income tax deduction for all military personnel (including retirees); and established a spouse employment program.

Mitch said in his January 16, 2007 *State of the State* address:

> "Indiana is a state of patriots. One sees it not just on Independence Day, Memorial Day, or Veterans Day but every day. When you hold my job, you see it most unforgettably at the funerals of the fallen. But our treatment of those who serve in uniform does not fully reflect the love and gratitude we feel for them. It does not match that of other states. Patriotism knows no party label; please join me in upgrading the way we support our soldiers, veterans, and the families who have sacrificed with them to protect the freedoms we all enjoy."

Many veterans had been working for years just to make progress on any one of these fronts, but to do so much so fast, was a windfall for many, to say the least. After the speech, one Democratic legislator said, "It was bipartisan, it was cooperative, and it was mutual. There will not be a state in America that expresses its reverence, its gratitude, its appreciation for the soldiers of today and yesterday, more than we will."

In 2011, Indiana moved up two places from eighth to sixth on *Site Selection* magazine's list of best states to do business. Going from eighth to sixth on a job creation list meant everyone should know without being told that the team was going to work immediately on cracking the top five and ultimately getting to number one. It meant finding out what the one-through-five best states had that Indiana did not.

In this case, not much. Indiana's regulatory and tax climates ranked among the best in the country, but Indiana was the only state out of the six that was not considered a Right to Work state. That all changed during the 2012 legislative session when the Governor, the Speaker of the House and the Senate President pro-temp ushered the bill through, making Right to Work the new law of the land, joining Indiana with twenty-two other states around the country.

Always aiming higher meant hundreds of new jobs, whether or not companies were willing to say publicly that Indiana's new union ruling was a factor in their decision to locate here.

No natural or manmade disaster is ever the same.

THIRTEEN

Great Leaders Do Not Fight the Next Battle Same As the Last

ALBERT EINSTEIN DEFINED INSANITY as doing the same thing over and over but always expecting a different result. If you want different results, you must look for what is not working and why. Your perspective on each issue, message and response must be objective, not reflexive, whether you are an incumbent or the challenger. Only after an honest survey of the competitive landscape will you be able to play it through without prejudice.

Obviously, this means you must be willing to alter your course with new information. Just as in battle, you must be able to adapt your campaign plan. It is the candidate who knows it all and ignores the demands of changing technology and the up-to-date electorate, who will be left behind in today's instant information-sharing. Change is constant. In the long run, ignoring new information means sacrificing resources and progress.

Technological advances are double-edged, to be sure. While new technology makes it easier to share, organize, deploy facts and marching orders, it also forces leaders to lead fast. Obtaining intelligence from the field via a hundred cell phones canvassing a single community, twitter blasts, video teleconferencing, and meet-ups online have expanded the playing field and increased the necessity of going after every vote.

Great leaders are voracious learners who never stop questing for more information and are not moored to the past. They are led by facts, not rumors or blind faith in someone else's reputation. Therefore, it is paramount to trust your team and to know that their research on any topic is solid, prior to spouting off about what you think.

Remember, you will rarely, if ever, have one hundred percent of all the information you need to make the toughest calls. If you are not learning from those surrounding you, it is time to retool the team. Everyone around you should know you are constantly taking the pulse, assessing the news of the day, and have multiple reference points. Healthy competition is a prerequisite to over-performing; it cannot be achieved if everyone is content.

Great leaders are also optimistic even when the going gets tough. I recall one time the going was really tough and a reporter asked Mitch how he kept on, setback after setback. Mitch's response reflected the essence of what being an optimist is all about. He replied, "I keep a sunny disposition and move on to the next challenge."

In addition to being funny, this response had another desired effect. It sent the message that Mitch was not tired of the race. In fact, it signaled that tomorrow would be a new day and there remained too much to be done to rest. Temporary setbacks are just that, temporary. You get past them.

The fastest way to demoralize the team is for the head of the organization to appear defeated for even a moment. True believers and staff will belly-crawl on hot coals for you, but the second they sense you have given up, they will too, and worse, they will talk about it.

Even after you reach out to build consensus around a direction you want to go, not everyone will agree with where you plan to take them. It can be easy to get angry, but do not stay angry forever. Even if you are proven right and they were not there for you, forgive them and move forward. This posture is healthy because it allows people to be with you seventy-five percent of the time, knowing that you respect their commitment, and give them latitude rather than demand all-or-nothing from them.

A common mistake is to think you will win the next campaign the same way you won the last one. Times change and so do the obstacles and opponents. In the first campaign, Mitch ran as the challenger against an incumbent. As a first-time candidate he had low statewide name identification. And, as a challenger you are typically running against someone else's record.

On the other hand, when you are the incumbent, you run on your record and more importantly the steps you will take next. It is common to see first-time incumbents revert back to the strategy that got them elected the first time or run for different offices the same way. Just as issues will be different, so will your responsibilities. As governor during the reelection campaign, Mitch had to run the state, but the important experiences were similar. For example, Mitch would visit flood victims whether he was a candidate or governor. He would attend high school basketball games as either candidate or governor. And he would offer an annual agenda before he assumed office and every year thereafter. While Mitch could not be on RV1 every day as he was during the first campaign, he kept up a hectic travel schedule, making sure he did not ignore any region of the state.

Staffing is much different for a challenger and incumbent. There is no need to maintain the same level of campaign staff as an incumbent. Rather, make sure your campaign staff gets along with key office staff. If tension or turf battles arise between the staffs, there will be mistakes and problems. The boss is responsible for all it. It is essential both staffs know that when the campaign manager makes a request, it is just as important and not-to-be-ignored as when the chief of staff asks for something, and visa versa.

How campaigns and companies use technology often makes the difference between success and failure. This is another reason to surround yourself with younger staff. I have never met a smartphone that outsmarted someone under twenty. If you have not downloaded the latest application to your smartphone, younger folks look at you as if you must enjoy struggling.

Companies pay big money to build interactive websites full of video content and last-minute updates because technology is so critical to success. For those who still believe blogs, Twitter and Facebook are fads, you are simply in denial about the ways business is done today. A campaign needs a tech person to keep computers, digital recording equipment and communication technology up and running every minute, and to teach veterans how to use their devices.

In the old days, scheduling an event meant that staff would call the host, get directions to and from point A to point B, type them, make copies, fax a copy to everyone involved and organize a travel binder. Today, simply say the address into your smart phone and you can pull up a map with directions on your personal screen.

Know what the job calls for and get it done.

Mitch and Becky, best governor and lieutenant governor in the country.

FOURTEEN

Surround Yourself With the Best Team; It is Your X-Factor

SURROUND YOURSELF WITH THE best staff; they will make you look good. One of the most important decisions a leader can make is who his teammates will be. When you start fresh, you have a responsibility to break the mold.

President Lincoln made a daring move in 1861, when he selected his team. It was a time of deep crisis for the country. Instead of asking close friends and advisors, he chose cabinet members based on leadership qualities and diversity in their views. Some of them were rivals and were said to hate each other. However, Lincoln's courageous and innovative "team of rivals" added an historic dimension to his presidency and to the healing of our divided nation.

Hire people who want to make friends, people who are not dividers, whiners, or complainers. Sign up "get-er-doners," not face-timers who want to be part of the scene, but do not really want to work. Hire folks who do not boast about how much money you have raised, made, or have. Others can do that and it is more intimidating if you understate it. Hire folks who appreciate spending time out-of-state and who are loyal to the cause you champion. Any organization must intimately know the customer, which demands constant outreach at the grassroots level.

Hire folks who will "hang together or surely will hang separately," as Ben Franklin said, and folks who will get along with one another in the bunker. Easier said than done once the bullets start to fly, but over time the office staff will evolve together. Always be on the lookout for what you need, not who is applying. Too often, organizations simply rehire familiar faces or promote their problems to a different area, usually out of sight.

Hiring transformative managers to run government and paying them well lowers turnover, maintains interest and focus, and gooses productivity for the cause. Many times, retirees who reenlist to get back in the game are best at this.

Be prepared to have someone on your team act as traffic cop and make sure each volunteer stays focused on his or her assignment. Some volunteers may have mixed motives or a personal agenda. For example, industry experts who raise money for your campaign may also hope to influence your policy proposals. Some grassroots volunteers, betting you will win, may be positioning themselves for a job after the election.

During the 2004 campaign, Daniels recruited the most diverse staff the state had ever seen. Each had his or her strengths and could be loosely grouped as follows:

The egg breakers.

Bill Oesterle, the co-founder and CEO of Angie's List, was growing his business across the country at the same time he was managing the first campaign. Bill was the ideal manager because he was owned by nobody and had only Mitch's interests in mind. In a business where favors are expected, the campaign was always about "elect Mitch and you get good government," never about making someone else's political future. Only someone like Bill could have endured and pulled it off.

Joel Silverman stepped away from his successful corporate life and agreed to reorganize the Indiana Bureau of Motor Vehicles. With zero emotion, he closed down multiple small branches that had lost money, had low traffic counts, poor layouts, or poor customer relations. The bottom line was that these branches were bad taxpayer values. Although much of the credit went to those who followed in Joel's footsteps, none of the success would have been possible without his initial leadership. Joel was a guy who did not need the job but knew Mitch would allow him to do his.

The experience counts group.

While having newcomers is critical, no task was more important than Mitch's selection of a running mate. We had over thirty people interested in or recommended to us to serve as lieutenant governor. At the end of the selection process, the no-brainer at the beginning turned out to be the no-brainer in the end. State Senator Becky Skillman had risen up in leadership and had significant earlier experience in local government as well. Having her wisdom and instincts proved invaluable over the years. In accepting the assignment, Becky became Indiana's first elected female lieutenant governor.

The friend who is willing to be a constructive contrarian.

It is essential to include a close friend who does not want a job at the end of the campaign. Mark Lubbers had known Mitch most of their adult lives, had previous press experience in the governor's office in the eighties, and agreed to mentor the staff. As a family friend, Mark would know things no one else on the staff ever could. He was the epitome of *not* a yes-man and someone who could privately tell the governor if he thought an idea was way off-track. Mark could provide critical analysis on the run and never relied on a paycheck to do it.

The non-government experience, non-politicos group.

When Mitch scrapped the old Department of Commerce for a new model, the Indiana Economic Development Corporation (IEDC), he signed up Pat Miller and Mickey Maurer to head the innovative new agency. In 1982, Pat Miller had co-founded a small company, starting with just $500 out of her garage in Fort Wayne. That company grew into a multi-million dollar enterprise in just three years called Vera Bradley. Mickey Maurer, a lawyer and entrepreneur extraordinaire, co-owned the *Indianapolis Business Journal,* among other interests. Mickey, who agreed to work for one dollar, once said he was "interested in cutting deals, not ribbons." The two entrepreneurial magnates revolutionized the way Indiana competed for jobs.

As number three and general counsel, Miller and Maurer groomed a younger talented attorney, Nate Feltman, who had spent time in Russia, working on international business deals. When Pat returned full-time to Vera Bradley, Mickey took over the IEDC. And when Mickey returned to his many businesses, Nate took the helm. For years, there was incredible continuity and the epitome of succession planning.

All stars – back from retirement.

The governor's second Chief of Staff, Earl Goode, was due to retire when he agreed to run the Department of Administration and reevaluate all state contracts. After the first Chief of Staff, Harry Gonso, returned to the private sector, Earl agreed to move over to the Governor's Office and remained longer than the average service time most governors received previously. Another example of someone not working for the paycheck but instead, doing it for all the right reasons. Earl's seasoned business skills, along with having no personal motives, defused more bombs just before they were about to go off than anyone I had ever seen.

Out-of-the-box thinkers.

Rick Thompson filmed all of the MitchTV episodes. His private-sector, reality-based eye, along with Mark Lubbers' knack for capturing Mitch's authenticity with, of course, zero retakes for a reality show, was an achievement no DC consultant could have delivered.

Policy wonks.

Most candidates go heavy on the political shop, producing talking- point memos that are comprised of nothing more than poll-tested bullet points. In a sense, we did just the opposite by hiring folks out of different private and public sector businesses and demanding they supply the blueprint in their area of expertise, such as Ryan Kitchell from Eli Lilly and Gina DelSanto from Butler University. The political shop played off the policy shop's lead. Once the two-step is mastered, the synergy multiplies your effectiveness on the campaign trail. The right foot knows where the left foot is throughout the entire dance.

Young, hungry and idealistic.

It is more important to hire folks driven by the cause, not the candidate, but a complete faith in the candidate will go a long way. The road crew, two recent college grads, Ben Ledo and Adam Horst, who traveled with Mitch the full sixteen months of that first campaign will forever hold a special place in everyone's hearts.

Trust, loyalty, work ethic.

These three qualities should be required of the people who surround you. A rare quartet of women worked with Mitch the duration of both terms and were a testament to hiring staff who believe in the cause and feed off constant high octane reform work. Maggie Ban was gatekeeper and scheduler, Betsy Burdick oversaw policy and agencies, Jane Jankowski served as press secretary. These three joined Mitch's staff after he was sworn in while Anita Samuel who worked on the first campaign ultimately served as the Governor's General Counsel. Most people in these roles do their jobs two years, not two terms

*Proving Ben would do anything for Mitch or let Mitch do anything
to Ben – the next Governor tries his hand at sheers.*

Governor high-fives the Nestle rabbit and the jobs landed in Anderson, IN.

FIFTEEN

Leave Something Lasting Behind

THE GREAT ONES LEAVE something lasting behind, even though they continually focus on the future. With the country and virtually every state facing monumental financial challenges, it is no time for the timid to take hold of the governmental reins. For a leader's message to resonate, everyday folks must know that their leader grasps the magnitude of what needs to be accomplished. Taking baby steps or tweaking a few details of the system is not sufficient. Today's challenges call for leaders to go in pursuit of equation changers.

Equation changers exponentially improve quality of life and by their very nature, leave something lasting behind. If you do not have a list of accomplishments you are leaving behind, then prepare to be seen as shortsighted because of your narrow scope of action and lack of focus on real people's needs. Leaving something lasting behind is evidence of your courage and vision in action, demonstrates your intelligent grasp of the urgency of solving problems and validates the logical step-by-step course of action you take to get results. Leaving something lasting behind reveals character and has nothing to do with ego.

Every day ripped off the calendar is a day gone forever and we all know history is recorded by those who demonstrate accomplishment. How each day is recorded is the difference between documented progress and time squandered. While a four-year term seems at the outset to be a long time, it really is not if you are planning to make a sea change, to turn the ship around and charge full-steam in another direction.

In Indiana, four years provides a governor the opportunity to craft only two budgets or four legislative sessions during which to conduct all necessary business. Because of this fact, Mitch exuded urgency, at times impatience. Picture a shot clock winding down from four to three to two to one year left in which to get everything done you can.

On the Governor's desk are decades of collected and inspired ideas. Some of these ideas are innovative and unique to the times, while others are acquired from researching best and worst practices around the country. Knowing best practices gets you caught up, but you must avoid worst practices. By studying them both, you will learn what to keep doing, start doing, and stop doing. Do not waste time reinventing the wheel if you do not have to.

Legacies are methodically developed over time and born out of equation changers, not from slick paid television commercials or by just showing up. PR campaigns fade. Do your job right and the way you are remembered will take care of itself.

There are various ways legacies can be created: physical assets built or produced; reshaping the organization's culture; and revitalization of the corporate or organizational outlook.

Creating a culture of pride.

Rich Lowry once wrote an article titled, "What Would Mitch Do?" One of Mitch's supporters actually made rubber bracelets stamped with WWMD because of his style of governing. Prior to Mitch, folks were not used to elected officials benchmarking, setting transparent goals, and then grading themselves. Because of his straightforwardness and results-oriented ways, voters became less cynical about people in government service. This type of leadership knows no age boundaries. Old and young alike can learn from a leader who is laser-focused on results and the future.

Many times veteran or senior party officials who want to stay in office are motivated to learn from others' leadership lessons. However, young leaders are more driven by a positive pragmatic approach. In 2011, Indiana Republicans elected three mayors and new city councilmen in their twenties. This next generation had been inspired by Mitch and stepped forward in spite of primary competition that included veteran politicians and folks who had supposedly waited their turn.

Changing the culture or reputation of any big organization is slow and can revert back more quickly than it improves, but positive cultural shifts provide an amazing force behind new outlooks and the mood of the people.

Another way to usher in pride is to honor your heritage and call attention to what it means to the future. If you visit soldiers overseas, do not just visit them, call their spouses when you get back and sincerely discuss how they are holding up, a practice Mitch has continued throughout his terms in office. The speed at which spouses at home call their friends and let them know the Governor just called is faster than the speed of light.

When he visited the Korean Demilitarized Zone on the fifty-sixth anniversary of the start of the Korean War, he laid an arrangement of white flowers by the plaque listing nine hundred Indiana soldiers who had lost their lives during the war. Mitch honored their past service, so that we may be reminded of it today.

Even rooting for your home team relates you to the citizen who may not be politically engaged but reads the newspaper. Daniels entered into a friendly wager with then Oklahoma Governor Brad Henry when the Indiana University Hoosiers faced the Oklahoma State University Cowboys in the 19th annual Insight Bowl on December 31, 2007. During the pre-game show, a few prominent folks were led out on the field to be introduced, including Mitch and T. Boone Pickens. As each was introduced, the crowd cheered respectfully and then went crazy when Pickens was named.

Mitch learned over and said, "I guess we know who won the applause meter."

Pickens replied, "For a hundred and sixty million, I better (bleep) win the applause meter!"

Regardless of the final score, voters appreciate you rooting for the home team and they remember it.

Scheduling other fun events that are not political at all sometimes have the greatest reach and connection. For example, back in April 2007, Mitch visited with the country's two oldest people, both Hoosiers. He celebrated Edna Parker's 114th birthday by honoring her with a Sagamore of the Wabash, one of the state's highest awards. "I bring you birthday greetings from everyone in the state. We're all so proud of you," Daniels told her. The governor and Mrs. Parker also met with Bertha Fry, 113, who came from her home in Muncie to the Heritage House Convalescent Center in Shelbyville. Members of both families and press were present for the historic meeting.

Every state or leader has different types of recognition he or she can award. Indiana governors used to freely pass out awards, a practice that lessened their value. When Mitch came into office, he stopped passing out awards like candy and started to carefully select those the state would honor. Once a year he bestowed the state's highest honor, the Sachem Award for civic leadership, on folks such as the late Jane Blaffer Owen, John Wooden, the Reverend Theodore M. Hesburgh, Bill and Gloria Gaither, Danny Danielson and Carl Erskine, all nationally known in their respective areas of expertise.

In addition to recognizing civic leaders, Mitch also started the practice of using one wall, now called the Hoosier Heritage Gallery, in his office on which he hung oil portraits of those who helped build Indiana. People honored in this manner, included: Harvey Weir Cook, Indiana's first flying ace in World War I; Mother Theodore Guerin, a teacher and saint; May Wright Sewall, a leader in the women's suffrage movement; Booth Tarkington, an author; Lew Wallace, a Civil War General and author; Madam C.J. Walker, an African American entrepreneur; William Henry Harrison, President, and Benjamin Harrison, President.

In addition to honoring past achievement, it is equally important to spotlight tomorrow's leaders. One tradition Mitch started was to recognize outstanding Hoosier high school students with Mr. and Miss Math and Science Awards. Many schools already awarded a Mr. and Miss Basketball, so why not in academics, too?

Servant leadership is, by definition, not about you. It is always bigger than you. Taking part in events like those described in this chapter reminds everyone of how timeless good works are. Of course, folks will long remember a leader who cut taxes, balanced the books and improved credit ratings, but nothing serves as an everyday reminder like a new bridge, highway or factory.

People take pride in roads and bridges that make everyday travel easier and safer. In just two terms, Mitch oversaw the construction of new bridges and multi-billion dollar road projects that had been promised for years in every quadrant in the state. The 2012 Milton-Madison Bridge, spanning the Ohio River between Indiana and Ohio, replaced an older, narrower version built in 1929. Transforming another region for years to come also included the construction of two new bridges at Jeffersonville. The three new bridges over the Ohio connected two states to accommodate the growth of a modern economy in these areas. These improvements had been talked about for decades, but were finally accomplished under Mitch.

People typically think that landing a new auto plant is winning the big prize in scoring new jobs and revenue. But in Indiana, diversification is the key. Hundreds of new companies that located in Indiana, including automobile plants such as Honda, had unique stories behind how and why they decided to plant their corporate flag in Indiana soil.

Mitch asked CEOs what was the deciding factor when they chose Indiana as the best place for their operation. The answers could have been five different reasons from five different companies. MEDCO liked the speed at which the state did its permitting, while other companies might have been convinced by the state's AAA credit rating or the ongoing improvements to our interstate access, roadways and bridges. Still others might have appreciated the low taxation rates or the new Right to Work law. Many times you do not know the reasons until a company decides to relocate, and that is why you must excel at everything you can control.

When you groom others to become successful, the wake you leave behind will continue to keep things stirred up. Throughout his career, Mitch had a soft spot for youngsters who needed a shot and were willing to work at it when given a chance to succeed. Turning around a student on a path to failure is an invaluable early investment.

Mitch was involved with helping children in a lot of different ways, including his participation in founding the Oaks Academy, a school for inner city youth; the Governor's Office internships and fellowships, and a group called Mitch's Kids, a partnership between the Governor and the Indiana Alliance of Boys & Girls Clubs that provided tutoring for children struggling with reading and math. Thousands of students between the ages five and fourteen benefitted from this program.

Mitch saw a need for intervention and felt strongly about revitalizing the mission of the old Indiana Soldiers' and Sailors' Children's Home and believed a better program could serve more at-risk youth and save the state money at the same time.

Privately founded in 1865, the Children's Home provided care and education to orphaned and destitute children of Civil War Union Army veterans. Two years later, the state assumed control, but over time, maintaining the facility became too costly and the small number of children served were not getting the education they needed. Mitch stepped in and pushed for a change.

The Hoosier Youth Challenge Academy, started by the governor in 2007, was being run by the National Guard at Camp Atterbury. In 2010, Mitch recommended moving this seventeen and one-half-month, two-phase, quasi-military program to the Children's Home, where more kids could be accepted. The training agenda was structured to give a second chance to at-risk teenagers between sixteen and eighteen years old. In May that year, a class of ninety young men and women graduated from the Challenge Academy's new quarters at the old Soldiers' and Sailors' Children's Home.

Mitch addressed the graduates, saying: "When you fall, it's always hard to pick yourself up. However your fall brought you here to Knightstown. You've stuck through it, and you picked up these life skills to move forward and be successful in society. You are Indiana's future."

Mitch believed in giving a second chance to anyone who was willing to work toward a better life. This was demonstrated when prison inmates in a work release program were asked to refinish all the woodwork in the Governor's office. They learned the skills in prison to restore the oak woodwork to its original beauty. The labor cost taxpayers nothing and materials were only $800.

Mitch told the workers that the results were "amazing...just stunning" at a reception held for them after completing the project. They sat at the Governor's massive boardroom table that was also built by prison woodworkers. The magnificent table features the ninety-two counties inlaid in different Indiana woods.

Meeting with the Governor was an inspiration to men preparing to go back into the world. One inmate said the project had helped him repay his debt to society. Another, who had learned to cut hair while incarcerated, said the work release program had straightened out his life. William was still trimming Mitch's hair at Red's Classic Barbershop in downtown Indianapolis at the time of this writing.

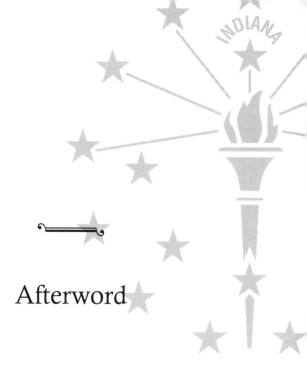

Afterword

MITCH RAISED INDIANA FROM near-bankruptcy during the most difficult economic times that any state had endured in generations. He raised expectations of what it meant to govern in the face of public anxiety and turmoil, and his leadership made him a man to watch and emulate.

Writing about a governor is pretty unusual but in Mitch's case, books, articles, analysis and commentary about his methods and success have been produced. A lot came out in print and on the air and internet when talking heads were speculating about whether or not he would run for President and if he did, what were his chances.

To all of that, I add this book about Mitch's journey as Governor to recreate the unique story of Indiana's comeback and to serve as a manual of steps and examples for aspiring leaders in government and business.

Mitch summarized it best in his 2010 *State of the State* address:

"A young seaman sought a veteran mariner's advice, asking, 'What do I do when I find myself in a gale force wind with a dangerous reef to leeward?' To which the old sea captain replied, 'What you do is, you don't get yourself in that position.' Through the discipline of legislators on this floor, and the superb, businesslike management of my colleagues in those balconies, Indiana stands in a position very different from virtually all our sister states. They crashed on the reef many months ago.

"They have seen their credit ratings downgraded and their borrowing costs soar. Indiana has a Triple-A credit rating for the first time ever, saving millions in interest costs for our cities, schools and universities. We will be using our carefully built reserves to get us through this next year and a half. Any reserves most other states had have long since disappeared.

"They have slashed, sometimes virtually halted, the construction and repair of state roads. In Michigan, they are grinding asphalt roads back into gravel, as though to regress by a century. But here, we are building for Indiana's future at a rate twice the previous all-time record. All over Indiana, the dreams of decades are becoming real: the Hoosier Heartland Corridor, the Fort to Port highway, US 31 from South Bend, I-69, and hundreds of others, all at full speed, under budget, ahead of schedule, taking shape before our eyes.

"After growing education spending five years in a row, by a total of twelve percent, we were recently, reluctantly forced to trim it, by some three cents on the dollar. But all across the country, education spending has been reduced by vastly more: by twice as much in places like Washington, Nebraska, and Connecticut; by three times as much in Virginia, Mississippi, and Utah; four times as much in Minnesota and South Carolina, six times as much in Alabama.

"Around our nation, states have closed parks, stiffed vendors, thrown people off Medicaid, stopped plowing snow, and released thousands of dangerous criminals from prison early. Overnight last night, the citizens of Iowa were protected by seven state troopers, total. We have done none of those things and don't intend to.

"Saddest of all, our sister states, at least forty of them, are doing the worst thing possible in times like these. They are raising taxes, adding to the burden on families already in distress, and making their economic climates even less attractive to new jobs than they were before. Michigan, Wisconsin, New Jersey and at least eleven more have raised income taxes. Ohio, Oregon, Minnesota, and thirty more have raised gas taxes. Many states have raised multiple taxes at the same time."

Because of the many successes Indiana achieved, Mitch was constantly asked the "what's next" question or more specifically, would he run for President? Whether or not he ever runs for another office, this book's purpose is to inspire other reform-minded citizens to run for office and get about the bold work ahead that is necessary to rebuild our nation.

These lessons prove it can be done and show how the nation can learn from Mitch Daniels. We all know what the problems are: that our country must deal with our debt, nuclear capability in unstable nations, an uncertain private sector, and the impact of world hunger. This guide provides some options for implementing ideas into action.

Indiana Rankings

• Indiana ranks best in the Midwest and fifth overall in *Area Development* magazine's Top States for Doing Business study.

• Indiana ranks sixth in the nation for its business climate according to *Site Selection* magazine.

• The Tax Foundation's 2012 Business Tax Climate Index ranked Indiana first in the Midwest and 10th nationally.

• As the 23rd right-to-work state, Indiana is the first state to enact such a law in 10 years and the only state in the mid-to-upper Atlantic region.

• Indiana has the lowest state government employment per capita of any state (U.S. Census Bureau, 2008 annual survey of public employment and payroll)

• Clean energy jobs grew by nearly 18 percent between 1998 and 2007, ranking Indiana first in the industrial Midwest in overall job growth in the clean energy economy. (Pew Charitable Trusts- June 2009)

• Indiana is ranked one of the top 15 lowest business cost locations in the country. (*Forbes* – September 2011)

• Indiana ranks first in the Midwest in the Milken Institute's most recent "Cost of Doing Business Index".

• Indiana is among the best states in the nation for business, ranking first in the Midwest and fifth nationally in *Chief Executive Magazine's* seventh annual "Best & Worst States" survey.

• Workers' compensation premiums rates are second lowest in the nation and lowest in the Midwest. (Oregon Department of Consumer & Business Services – May 2011)

• Indiana ranks 5th in the nation for its business tax and regulatory climate according to the *Enterprising States* study by the U.S. Chamber of Commerce and National Chamber Foundation.

• Indiana has the third-freest economy in the U.S. according to the "Freedom in the 50 States" study by the Mercatus Center.

• The Indiana Bureau of Motor Vehicles received the International Customer Service Excellence Award for excellence twice, becoming the first-ever two-time recipient. (AAMVA – July 2008, October 2010)

• Indiana's Telecommunications Deregulation Act has made the state a national leader in telecom reform.

• Indiana was recognized by two national organizations, The United States Public Interest Research Group (US PIRG) and the Sunshine Review, for the state's efforts to bring more transparency to government.

• Indiana's record-breaking nationally recognized Major Moves 10-year infrastructure improvement program has funded more than 200 major roadway and bridge projects and produced the longest contiguous road construction project in the country.

• Indiana now has the third most E85 gasoline pumps of any state.

• Indiana is one of the nation's fastest wind growth states and remains the largest provider of wind power east of the Mississippi.

What Others Are Saying About Mitch Daniels

Andrew Romano, *Newsweek:* "Indiana Gov. Mitch Daniels is the model of a creative Reality-Based Republican. He has insured 50,000 low-income Hoosiers through a budget-neutral combination of health savings accounts and catastrophic coverage. He's lowered property taxes, transformed a $600 million deficit into a $1 billion surplus, and launched a public-works program with $4 billion raised from privatizing the state's toll road. He is pro-life and pro-green, but not shrilly so. With Wisconsin Rep. Paul Ryan, Louisiana Gov. Bobby Jindal, and Virginia Governor-elect Bob McDonnell, Daniels points the way toward a future in which Republicans stop ignoring reality —and start working to improve it."

Jeb Bush, PolitiJax (blog post): "Mitch is the only one who sees the stark perils and will offer real detailed proposals."

J. Reihan Salam, Forbes.com: "If Republicans are ever going to make a comeback, they need to make the case against never-ending bailouts of the rich and connected. The right man for the job is Mitch Daniels, the governor of Indiana."

House Republican Leader, Rep. John Boehner: "Governor Daniels has emerged as one of our nation's leading voices for reform and common sense in government.

Rich Lowery, *National Review:* "More than any other Republican officeholders, Daniels points the way ahead."

Chris Cillizza, *The Washington Post:* "Daniels…shows that he is a force to be reckoned with in the reshaping of the Republican Party."

John Aloysius Farrell, *US News & World Report:* "Daniels is exactly the kind of Republican that could woo independent voters and conservative Democrats- maybe even young folks – back to the GOP 2012."

David Broder, *The Washington Post*: "The one-time Reagan White House political director and Bush White House budget chief is not your run-of-the-mill intellectual. His style is to be down-home, but his record of accomplishment is dazzling."

George Will, December 25, 2011, on "This Week" responding to Christiane Amanpour's question about his biggest political disappointment of the year: "About 11 o'clock at night on Saturday, May 21st, I got a call from my friend, the governor of Indiana, saying that the next morning he was going to announce he – Mitch Daniels – was not going to run for president. The man best suited by experience, temperament and philosophy opted out."

About the Author

On election night, 2008, Governor Daniels said, "Eric Holcomb, you hoss. Eric, when I thank you, I am thanking thousands of people who ran the kind of campaign we said Indiana deserved, clean and positive all the way. And in all excitement, the rightful excitement about the presidential election, it was easy for some folks to miss the biggest grassroots organization in Indiana history that was the one you put together in this election, and I can't thank you enough."

"The Best Gubernatorial Campaign of 2008." Chris Cillizza, "The Fix," *The Washington Post*

Mitch Daniels (R-IN), the "Best-Run Governor's Campaign" of the 2008 election. *Politics Magazine.*

"We don't expect a formal announcement, but a hint sure would be nice. One thing is certain, with over 1,000 people paying thousands of dollars to attend, Indiana Republican Party Chairman Eric Holcomb is a fundraising genius." Capitol & Washington (blog post)

Frank Donatelli credited Indiana Republican Party Chairman Eric Holcomb with convincing GOPAC to come to Indy, saying, he is "a superb promoter of the results Republicans have achieved in Indiana and how their success can be a model for other states." Tom Beven, *Real Clear Politics*

Eric Holcomb currently serves as the Indiana State Republican Chairman and was Governor Mitch Daniels' deputy chief of staff and campaign manager. He worked for Mitch from day one of his gubernatorial journey and has more than enough behind-the-scenes experience; success in campaign, organizational and grassroots strategy; political acuity; generosity of spirit, and downright heart to write this book.

Eric regularly advises conservative organizations, such as the Republican Governor's Association and the Republican National Committee, as well as Republican candidates around the country. A familiar guest speaker at Indiana conferences, civic groups and professional associations, he is also a regular at Party events throughout Indiana. He is well-known in the national political community and has authored winning campaign plans on the national, state and local levels.

Eric Holcomb receiving county vote totals on election night, 2004.